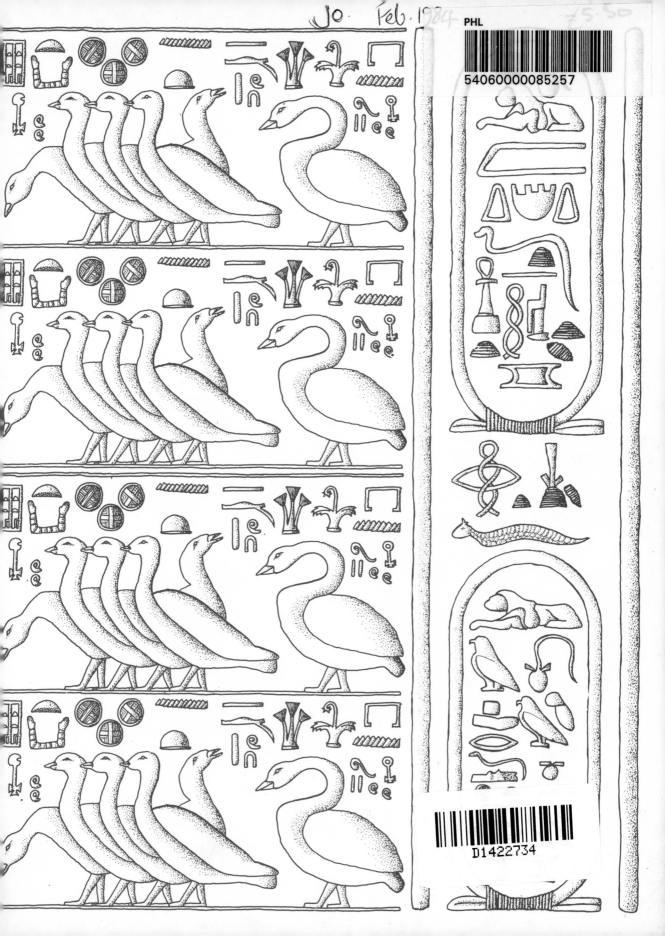

ROMER'S EGYPT

IN MEMORIAM

SO·THE·HEART·BE·RIGHT

Joanna Defrates

1945-2000

ROMER'S EGYPT

A New Light on the Civilization of Ancient Egypt

JOHN ROMER

MICHAEL JOSEPH/RAINBIRD

First published in Great Britain 1982 by
Michael Joseph Ltd,
44 Bedford Square, London WC1 and
The Rainbird Publishing Group Ltd,
40 Park Street, London W1Y 4DE
who designed and produced the book

ISBN: 0 7181 2136 8

Design: Nigel Partridge
Production: Elizabeth Winder

Text set by SX Composing Ltd
Rayleigh, Essex, England
Colour originated by
Hongkong Graphic Arts Service
Printed and bound by
Toppan Printing Company, Singapore

CONTENTS

PREFACE
AND
ACKNOWLEDGMENTS

Ancient Egypt is two different things: the monuments that hold the physical reality of the ancient world, and the product of a modern science built from the theories and researches of generations of scholars and curators. I hope that the title of this book suggests not incipient megalomania but rather that the book contains a personal selection of information, opinions and pictures about ancient Egypt – a balance between an appreciation of the monuments themselves and a description and investigation of some of the theories that have been held about them. The book also deals with what, it seems to me, a modern person wants to know: the hows and whys of the ancient monuments and the people who made them – each chapter intended as a preface to a different aspect of the ancient society.

Although its themes have been fitted around the general patterns of the ancient country's political and economic development, the text does not adhere to a strict chronological order of events, nor have I given equal weight to all periods of the ancient history. To have done so would have diffused the subject matter through descriptions of millenia of courtly politics. Conversely, I felt that a completely non-historical approach would run the risk of distorting the underlying motivations of the ancient society, giving the impression that the ancient Egyptians were simple folk who spent their time happily sawing away at statues and coffins, weirdly preoccupied with death and the invention of some of its more bizarre fittings.

Traditionally, egyptologists have considered that the ancient language was the primary key for the understanding of the ancient people and so, by the very nature of most of the ancient texts, their work has been very much a study of public lives. However, during the past twenty years, Egyptian archeology has been enlivened by new areas of research that have not only resulted in a fresh vision of the ancient society but also an awareness that much of the information basic for an understanding of the ancient culture has still to be gathered from its sites. It is now recognized as a serious weakness of the subject that, for example, not one large town site typical of urban life in those times has ever been scientifically excavated;

that the vital records of private lives – the realities of social and economic history – have until quite recently, been largely ignored, many earlier scholars simply drawing on their own experiences in contemporary societies to fill this considerable gap in their knowledge. It is some of the results of these recent researches into the more practical aspects of history that form a part of the subject of this book – new information that has already profoundly affected many of the older interpretations of the ancient Egyptian civilization.

I have also attempted to de-mystify many of the little-discussed, but nonetheless fascinating, aspects of ancient Egyptian culture. With an understandable impulse to protect their studies from vulgarization and mis-interpretation, specialists have frequently guarded their work with a shield of sometimes paralysing pedantry. This, unfortunately, has often effectively barred the way to more general knowledge of some of the finest ancient literature and art. Thwarted in their ambitions to discover more about the ancient Egyptians, many have turned to explanations of this culture which, though perhaps less credible than those of the specialists, are certainly more amusing and are, at least, the product of modern, if delinquent, minds.

Two more points; first, I have treated the powerful ancient attitudes to myth and ritual as being beyond rationalization – in the sense that all faiths are, by nature, not amenable to such explanations. Surprisingly, perhaps, some parallels to the ancient attitudes may still be found in modern society; when, for example, an RAF chaplain blesses the 'hieroglyph' signifying a recently qualified pilot's achievement – the 'wings' newly sewn onto his uniform; the elaborate rituals of weddings and coronations; the simple rite of offering flowers at the graves or cenotaphs of our own dead. For its comprehension, ancient belief must be allowed an equal credibility.

Second, it should be pointed out that there are always great problems of terminology lurking in general discussions of ancient societies. While, for example, the contemporary architect usually designs complete environments, the term 'architect' that is sometimes used to describe the work of some ancient officials seems to relate more to the modern position of project supervisor. In ancient Egypt, tradition and ritual requirement usually supplied the forms that our architects have had to invent for themselves. Thus, modern terms used to describe many different aspects of the ancient society can hold slightly different implications, or subtle changes of meaning, from the images that they usually evoke in contemporary society.

--- ◆ ● ◆ ---

Similar spacers occur irregularly throughout this book. They do not denote the passing of time nor expurgations of erotic or libellous material but have been used simply to allow the presentation of separate aspects of one chapter's general subject: a method of dividing it so that each section is, in some measure, a footnote to the other.

It is a custom of BBC TV documentaries that the production teams do not appear in the finished product. Six people, however, went to Egypt to make the three films of 'Romer's Egypt' (these following 'Diary of a Search', which had been made some time before). When we climbed the Great Pyramid of Giza, I had only to drag myself up – cameraman Martin Patmore also had to take his cine camera, while his assistant Trevor Vincent carried the tripod, lenses and extra rolls of film, and the soundman Bruce Galloway his tape recorders and microphones. All worked as they climbed. With us was Rita Cooper, surely the most patient of all production assistants, and Paul Watson, the producer whose idea it was, of course, to climb the pyramid in the first place! As director he also had the unenviable task, among a mountain of other responsibilities, to ensure that I spoke with no more than my usual incomprehensibility. For their separate and combined excellence I owe them a great deal.

As part of an attempt to avoid the quite erroneous quality of omnipotence with which many television documentaries seem to be imbued, my commentaries to camera were usually only briefly rehearsed and were not composed as written texts. Such spontaneity, however, brought its own problems, though these were brilliantly resolved in the London cutting rooms by film editor Peter Symes, and Paul Watson. Time and time again, Paul encapsulated verbal ideas in beautiful sequences of film that 'said' more in less time than ever a presenter could have done.

Apart from the historical texts, which have been taken from Breasted's splendidly biblical renderings (amended slightly in order to simplify), most of the translations quoted in this book are from Miriam Lichtheim's *Ancient Egyptian Literature* (published by the University of California Press) and I am most grateful to be able to use the results of such sympathetic scholarship. The translation of the speech of Hermes Trismegistus with which the book starts and finishes, is A. D. Noak's taken from *Coptic Egypt* (ed. John D. Cooney and published by The Brooklyn Museum, 1944). My description of the changing environment of the Nile Valley in ancient times is based, in part, on Karl Butzer's *Early Hydraulic Civilization in Egypt*, arguably the single most significant work of the 'new' egyptology. The brief extracts from *Amduat* are the translations of Alexandre Piankoff (*Egyptian Religious Texts and Representations*: Bollingen Series 40; Copyright © 1957–1974 by Princeton University Press. Extract reprinted by permission of Princeton University Press) from whose publications I have benefited in many different ways. Additionally, I should like to thank the estates of Ezra Pound and T. S. Eliot, their British publisher Faber and Faber, and their American publishers, New Directions

Publishing Corporation, and Harcourt Brace Jovanovich Inc., respectively, for allowing me to reproduce two brief quotations from their works on pages 85 and 175. Further details of all these works are to be found in the Bibliography. I should also record here my especial debt to my editor Peter Coxhead, who has laboured long with a difficult manuscript.

The content of both TV films and book also owes a great deal to conversations with colleagues in Egypt, Europe and the USA, and if they recognize their thoughts served up under new guises I beg their indulgence. But most of all, I am under a special obligation to my Egyptian friends and colleagues in Cairo and Luxor, who are always such very good hosts.

The term predynastic has been used to describe all the specifically Egyptian cultures that existed in Egypt before the rise of the First Dynasty. The ancient dates are drawn, in the most part, from the second edition of the *Cambridge Ancient History*. The chronological table and the map of Egypt are designed solely to place the reader in time and space within the context of the material presented in this book.

I have taken the photographs used to illustrate this book over the past fifteen years. Visitors to the same places today might well find some of them changed, either in the course of the very rapid progress that has taken place in Egypt during this period or, more simply, by the 'hand of time'. Today the Egyptian authorities valiantly safeguard and conserve the remains of a civilization which, with its near four-thousand-year span of remains, seems to overwhelm by its sheer quantity. Yet, as we might well find to all our costs, ancient Egypt is a finite commodity and, excavated, studied and visited now by people from all over the world, its continuing survival should concern us all.

John Romer
Aiola, Tuscany 1982

CHAPTER ONE

CATARACTS AND NILOMETERS

Most of Egypt is a desert. It will preserve almost anything that is buried in it but virtually nothing will grow there. The ancient Egyptians went to this desert to hunt and to quarry its beautiful hard stones; and they used its edges for their cemeteries. Only a handful of people actually lived in the desert. Like the modern Egyptians, the ancients lived alongside the river that provided them with water and the soil in which they grew their crops. Then, as now, the country of Egypt could be accurately described, as it was by the Greek historian Herodotus nearly two-and-a-half thousand years ago, as the Gift of the Nile.

Around ninety-five per cent of the land of Egypt has been a desert for more than 30,000 years – not the vast tracts of golden sands that roll, in the popular imagination, from the Atlantic coast to the Red Sea, but desolate regions of plains and mountains, of rocks and boulders shattered by terrible extremes of hot and cold in a desiccated landscape punctuated by dunes of wind-blown sand. The longest river in the world cuts down through this desert from south to north to create the Nile Valley. The sediments carried by the river have made a deltaic region where the river enters the Mediterranean: a huge fan-shaped plain of even-grained black silt more than one hundred miles long and nearly two hundred miles across, that slopes gently down some fifty feet on its way to the edge of the sea. It was, however, the valley that was the cradle of the ancient civilization, a great sheltered oasis that runs like a single furrow some 625 miles long from the ancient southern border of the country to the beginnings of the Delta close by modern Cairo. To stand on the edges of the desert above them, the ancient Egyptians climbed the cliffs that fringed their valley, and this high hostile area they called *Dashre*, the 'Red Land'. To return to their homes they descended to *Keme*, the 'Black Land' – an ancient name for the valley that holds the Nile silt.

At Aswan the Nile breached a ridge of dull-red granite in a marvellous

Nile Valley at Thebes: a thin cliff-bordered oasis – the ancient Egyptian environment. In the foreground are the ruins of an unfinished temple of the Middle Kingdom

Ancient limestone quarries at western Thebes

Rich vegetation growing in the Nile silt. Elephantine Island, Aswan

froth of white-water rapids. Beyond this cataract lay the wild Sudan and a largely unknown Africa. Some forty miles north of Aswan, at Silsila and Silwa, the river again breached rocky barriers – this time of sandstone – before it gracefully widened into the great limestone valley that is typical of much of the Egyptian landscape. Since ancient times the Nile has moved westwards across the valley floor, sometimes by as much as three miles, and today the path of the river has been straightened out, its flow slowed by the dams at Aswan. However, the landscape of the valley is still essentially what it was some 4,000 years ago at the height of its ancient prosperity.

Not only did the Greeks dub Egypt as the Gift of the Nile, but they also responded to the uncanny, almost fantastic, orientations of its simple landscape. 'Do you not know, O Asclepius, that Egypt is the copy of Heaven, or rather, the place where here below are mediated and projected all operations which govern and actuate the heavenly forces? Even more than that, if the whole truth is to be told, our land is the temple of the entire World.'

This quiet wide river, fringed by bright green fields and sheltered by the straight limestone cliffs, was the root of the ancient Egyptian experience. Outside the valley lay a world of disorder, wild beasts, and strange formless lands with none of the predictable orientations of the great valley, the most individual topography in the world, where the course of the river, in a virtually two-dimensional landscape, bisects the path of the sun above it. This sun and the river landscape are at right angles to each other, and on the main points of the compass. The sun rises from behind the eastern cliffs and sets beyond the cliffs on the opposite side of the valley. And this basic geometry exists in a hot well-watered luxuriance that is one of the richest agricultural regions of the world. The movement of the life-giving forces through this veritable hot-house was constant, endless, in a land whose elements functioned like the vibrations in a quartz crystal, through the points of the compass, through the earth and sky.

Every year the great river flooded the valley. Monsoons that hit the Abyssinian highlands during the months of July and August fed the river's southern tributaries and caused the Nile to burst its banks and cover the parched fields. The huge flood also carried silts that were spread across the fields in a remarkable annual process of fertilization. These deposits, over the millenia, have become the soil of the black fields spread over the white limestone of the valley floor. When this annual flood receded it exposed a plain of shiny mud, its fecund potential symbolized by pools of water filled with silvery fish which, as the remaining water slowly evaporated, were crowded even closer together. The great flood gave ancient Egypt its three annual seasons: Inundation, Winter (spring), and Summer. The gaps in this simple agrarian calendar of flood, growth, harvest and drought left the large labour force with months of relative inactivity.

In their endless repetitions, in the claustrophobic exuberance of this river oasis set below a sterile desert and amid strong bandings of verticals and horizontals that formed the landscape, the environment was as rhythmic as the sun and the river. Harmonious rhythms that set the ancient Egyptians into a uniquely ordered world which, not surprisingly, produced a race that was itself extraordinarily ordered, and insistant on the virtues of constancy, integrity, and clarity – all attitudes that are apt to produce a rich and stable society. In ancient Egypt they produced a society that was so stable and so rich that it had time for a good deal more than hunting for food and propitiating savage gods as many of its contemporaries were doing elsewhere in their less regulated environments.

In this model paradise, using the simplest system of winter agriculture, the ancient Egyptians cultivated wheat, flax, and vegetables, and grazed cattle and sheep on the fallow and marshy lands. And along the reeded river banks they hunted game, wildfowl, fish, even hippopotami. While the diet of the peasants was probably quite limited – consisting mainly of bread, onions and beer – the well-to-do lived very well indeed.

Earlier generations of historians, perhaps fired by the British irrigation projects in Egypt of the last century, described the ancient kings as masters of vast irrigation systems and drainage canals: the organizers of national prosperity. It has even been suggested that this high level of hydraulic control was itself the basis of the ancient system of government, which is a virtual inversion of the ancient view that the good order of the Egyptian state was due to the king, who was its embodiment and responsible for its prosperity. In reality, the ancient agricultural system was not organized on a national level until the last phases of its ancient history. The ancient irrigation technology was very simple and seldom changed. Even the smallest of innovations, such as the introduction during the Late Period of the water wheel, brought spectacular increases in both acreage and crop yields. But even without such simple technology, the 'Black Land' was fat enough to support its people with an ease that was not common in the ancient world.

Despite their prosperity, the ancient Egyptians were, in most things, a moderate and careful nation. Plutarch, a Greek who visited Egypt during the first century after Christ, tells us that the priests at the temples of the capital, Memphis, did not like the sacred bulls to grow fat, 'nor themselves, either; but rather they desired that their bodies, the encasement of their souls, shall be well adjusted and light, and shall not oppress the divine element by the predominance and preponderance of the mortal'. How well the ancient Egyptians succeeded is apparent today from an examination of their mummies. These show that although deficiency diseases were probably present in the population, most people obtained at least adequate nourishment. Like people today, some of the ancient Egyptians suffered from obesity and bad teeth. Some of them greatly enjoyed feasts, highly organized marathons of eating and drinking, and there are many splendid observations on these activities in the ancient paintings and texts. Perhaps it was because of this gourmandizing that gout and arterio-sclerosis have been detected in the ancient mummies, though many other endemic hazards of our modern civilization do not seem to have been around. Conversely, there may have been other afflictions that have since disappeared, for the symptoms of several presently unknown diseases are described in some detail by ancient physicians.

Even with these hazards of the flesh, it is apparent that the ancient Egyptians inhabited a relatively idyllic world – a world that also provided a well-defined stage for the activities of ancient gods. Everyday the sun god, Re, was reborn on the eastern horizon and crossed the blue Egyptian sky to descend into the western underworld – the realm of the dead where he began his nightly voyage of resurrection through the darkness. And it was gods of fertility and fecundity that, every year, made the river rise and flood. Although these regular rhythms of the land and the river created a nation that loved good order and symmetry, there were, inevitably, some elements of randomness in their lives, and these the ancient Egyptians sought to control and encompass by ordered rites and rituals.

The most obvious erratic and unique event of human existence is, of course, death, and the ancient Egyptians expended more energy than any other nation to assimilate this single inevitable event into the natural rhythm of death and rebirth that was all around them. Indeed, the marvellous monuments made by the ancient Egyptians for their dead – the pyramids, the painted tombs, coffins, sculpture and all the rest – have succeeded in making them immortal; as they intended their names are 'living for ever'.

Like death, historic events are also unique and it is to be expected, therefore, that the ancient Egyptians recorded their political history as a series of recurrent patterns that stress the elements of repetition – much to the annoyance of many modern historians who are interested in exactly the opposite. The ancient scribes' descriptions of wars against other nations, for example, tend to follow the same narrative, and all have the same result. Victory was inevitable for the king of Egypt in the eyes of his people and, thanks largely to the country's isolated position in the ancient world, such interpretations of events were seldom contradicted by uncomfortable realities.

There was, however, one element in this hermetically sealed universe that was neither constant nor could it be contained by rites, rituals or dogmas. This was drought, and on its coming it shattered the centre of the ancient society. This single weakness was the generator of a great deal of speculation about the ephemeral nature of this world and of the permanence and dreadful inevitability of death. Occasional and devastating fluctuations in the volume of the annual flood dramatically affected food

*Granite rocks of the Aswan Cataract bearing the white markings of
the old flood levels of the Nile*

supplies. Rainfall in Egypt was never sufficient to maintain even a minimum of level vegetation. Low flood levels, therefore, were the proof of the existence of good and bad in nature and in its gods. It gave a raw edge to the ancient faith and a spur to ritual correctness and conservatism.

At points down the river from Aswan to the Mediterranean were nilometers – passages that led down to the river, marked with fixed gauges to measure the river's height. In good years these measurements were used to calculate the levies that were extracted from the landowners and peasants by the royal exchequers. Traditionally, the great river started its rise on 15 July, the ancient New Year's Day. First, the greenish waters from the eastern tributaries poured down the river and washed through the nilometers. They were then joined by the reddish iron-oxide-rich waters of the White Nile from the western tributaries and the flood, ever rising, was watched anxiously and measured by the priests. It usually reached its full height in September when the entire country was inundated and only the towns and temples, built on high mounds or protected by dykes, stood above the glass-like waters. It was a sight of great beauty, but not seen since 1966, when the High Dam at Aswan started to contain the entire annual inundation in its great lake, allowing the parcelling out of the flood waters around the year as they are needed. What a profound and revolutionary change for a nation that, since the beginnings of its history, saw its life's blood in this annual flooding!

The ancient Egyptians took the awesome flood to be the result of dramas that were taking place in the mysterious pits and pools at the centre of the world. Nun, the elemental god that personified moisture, gave his bounty to his children who spread it throughout Egypt: the corpse of the great god Osiris gave its amazing fertilizing powers to the water, the land and its crops. Hapy was the Nile god himself, plump, full-breasted and coloured like the floodwaters 'whose arrival brings joy to everyone, nourishes the fields, finds provender for all of Egypt'.

Typically, the river rose a maximum of some thirty feet above its normal height at Aswan, some twenty feet close by modern Cairo and about half that height in the Delta. But if the priests at the nilometer at Aswan registered a floodwater height that was six feet below the normal, famine would inevitably spread throughout Egypt and the crop would be reduced in many parts of the valley by as much as three quarters. Prospects would dramatically worsen if the floodwaters remained low for several successive years. Drainage patterns in the fields would change, the area of land potentially available for cultivation would, therefore, shrink and the stranded fields would lie arid under the sun until abnormally high flooding would bring the water to them again.

Levels six feet above usual at Aswan could be equally disastrous for the ancient economy. Dykes would be breached and the flood would destroy the vulnerable mud-brick domestic architecture and flood the stone temples. Seed stores might be damaged, potential crop levels thereby being reduced. The delay in sowing, caused by a lengthy period of flooding would mean that later in the year the crops would roast under the hot summer sun. And these late crops were also liable to high levels of infestations by all manner of blights and insects that had thrived during the increased period of dampness.

So although the land of Egypt could be a pastoral paradise, the ancient society existed on an ecological knife edge – always there was the chance of a potential disaster. In the long term, population size and, indeed the fate of the nation, was dictated by the river and its floods.

The pattern created by the behaviour of the river was one of long stable periods punctuated by intermediate years of drought or overflooding – eras of hardship, anarchy and starvation. These intermediate periods are graphically described in a series of moralizing texts that are some of the most profoundly introspective writings to have survived from ancient times. They were written, apparently later than the events that they describe, to serve as warnings against the terrors of disorder and irreligiousness. When all was right with their land the Egyptians believed that the natural harmony had come from the rites and rituals of their religion which had united men and gods for their mutual benefit and satisfaction.

Overleaf *The west bank of the Nile at Es-Sabaiya near Aswan on an October evening*

By combining the fragmentary descriptions of the state of the country-side in those moralizing lamentations with the scanty contemporary records of the flood levels it has been possible to discover something about the most dramatic effects of the fluctuating river. This rather novel interpretation of ancient Egyptian history has recently received considerable support from geographical studies on the great lakes and rivers of East Africa and the southern Sahara – regions that are close to, and sometimes part of the vast drainage basin of the Upper Nile. These studies have demonstrated that enormous fluctuations of water level took place in those regions at times that closely correspond with the periods of prosperity and decline in ancient Egyptian history.

This view of ancient history is curiously paralleled by the present global situation. The 'energy crisis' has been caused, so one might say, by the realization in the oil-producing countries of the limits of their natural resources. Although this has resulted in endless political consequences right around the world, it is the environment, as it was in ancient Egypt, that has provided the ultimate parameters of the debate: the geographical and geological facts that have provided the political consequences.

The prosperity enjoyed by the Egyptians was not, therefore, the result of a careful harnessing of the available natural resources in the manner of a modern technological fable that starts with a 'primitive' technology which is slowly improved but was, in fact, at the whim of geographical and meteorological factors. These brutally controlled the size of the population in the same way that a natural ecology is controlled by climate and disease. But the ancient Egyptians believed the reverse of this modern analysis and put man and his gods at the centre of the Universe. How they regarded the king – the single link between man and the gods – when, for example, he failed to deliver the goods and when the Nile did not flood properly, can only be guessed. Perhaps then they said they had no king. By careful conservation measures, by controlling the distribution of wheat stocks or initiating projects to dig canals and dykes to control and contain the flood waters available, the administration could, of course, partially offset the effects of low flooding levels in the short term. But a continued scarcity of water and lack of seed would inevitably drag the economy down: so rapidly that, as one writer has observed, even the proverbial seven lean years would certainly have brought national ruin. Subsequently, it would have taken optimum flood levels to get the country back on its feet.

These cycles of catastrophe and plenty usually took place over periods of hundreds of years but by emphasizing this overall pattern one quickly looses the realities of the ancient Egyptian life – a stable society living in an agrarian world. However, such broad generalizations are useful to grasp something of the span of ancient Egyptian history and to understand some of the underlying motivations and fears of the ancient nation. The chronological system that is traditionally used to divide this vast history is, in itself, ancient, having been invented by an Egyptian temple priest named Manetho who lived in the third century B.C. Manetho divided his country's history into thirty dynasties of kings, some of which have remained merely lists of otherwise unknown royal names which are, one suspects, largely literary devices for indicating the periods of hardship and national dissolution: the intermediate periods between the three great Kingdoms. Manetho's other dynasties, however, are composed of the names of famous kings – the rulers who were on the throne for long periods and whose names appear carved into the stone monuments that they caused to be built. Thus, the list accurately reflects the times of the Nile's

*Colossal statues of Amenhotep III standing amid the flood waters of
the last inundation. Western Thebes, 1966*

plenty and the times of drought, though they are expressed by Manetho in terms of their political consequences. Here, the list is brought to its conclusion at a later date than the lifetime of the temple priest, when Egypt was invaded by Arab armies which finally brought the ancient civilization in Egypt to its end.

ROYAL DYNASTIES	ELAPSED TIME (years)	DATES (B.C.) (approximate)	NAME OF PERIOD
	600	5200–4600	Early Predynastic
	1500	4600–3100	Late Predynastic (including Nagada culture)
I & II	414	3100–2686	Archaic
III–VI	505	2686–2181	Old Kingdom
VI–XI	190	2181–1991	First Intermediate
XII	205	1991–1786	Middle Kingdom
XIII–XVII	219	1786–1567	Second Intermediate
XVIII–XX	482	1567–1085	New Kingdom
XXI–XXX	743	1085–342	Late
XXXI	10	342–332	Persian
(Macedonian)	302	332–30	Ptolemaic (from 323)
(Roman Emperors)	343	30–A.D. 311	Greco-Roman
(Byzantine Emperors)	329	A.D. 313–A.D. 624	Coptic (Christian)

Recent studies have shown that before Manetho's dynasties began there was a long period of bountiful Niles, but during the Old Kingdom there was a decline in the flood levels which is now estimated to have been about thirty per cent. This gradual diminution of the natural resources meant that when the flood failed briefly, at the beginning of the First Intermediate Period, it had an immediate and devastating effect on the nation, which took nearly two hundred years to regain national prosperity during the Middle Kingdom. The revitalization of the country at that time was, apparently, greatly helped by a series of especially high floods which unblocked water courses that had long silted up, allowing the flood water to return to areas that had not been cultivated for a long time. It is probable that these same high flood levels, continuing over a long period, eventually brought the prosperity of the Middle Kingdom to its end. The next era of plenty was the brilliant New Kingdom, and this was impoverished by another disastrous succession of low Niles that hit the country during the 12th century B.C., perhaps during the reign of Ramesses III. Written records of that time show several different aspects of the national economic decline that was taking place; one of the most telling being the soaring inflation of the price of grain in the failing economy.

Estimates of the population sizes during these periods show us other aspects of the overall picture. During the three great Kingdoms the population of Egypt rose steadily from an estimated 870,000 in 3000 B.C. to more than three times that number around 1250 B.C. Because the ancient system of agriculture was more suited to the parts of the Nile valley where the flood plain was narrow, the regions where flooding was at its widest were not so densely populated. The most heavily populated areas, in a relatively empty country, were between Aswan and Kuft in the south, and in the area of the pyramid towns and the capital, Memphis, in the north of the valley. The large Delta region remained less populated than the Nile valley until the first millenium B.C., when the political centre of the country moved to the north. There is evidence that the process of settling these less densely populated areas, already well underway before the First Dynasty, was retarded by the centralization of the state under the king. Conservative estimates of the population of modern Egypt are around 38 million people, some parts of the country being among the most densely populated regions of the world: this is, obviously, very different from ancient times.

CHAPTER TWO

EARTH AND MOISTURE

The ancient Egyptians had many different ideas about how their world had been created and most of these started with water: the primeval waters of chaos, dark and formless. And in the midst of these waters a mound of earth arose, like the hillocks that appeared in the flooded fields as the Nile's inundation subsided. This muddy mound was the stage for the dramas of creation and for the making of the gods who were the sky, the earth, the atmosphere; for the coming of the sun and of vegetation – all the elements, in fact, that made up the ancient world.

This mound was, therefore, a central image for the ancient Egyptians and they never doubted that the mythical events that took place on it had brought their world into being. So potent was the black silt that appeared shining from beneath the receding flood waters that it was held to have the power to create life spontaneously, a belief that is still held in remote areas of rural Egypt. The story that the fields of Egypt were 'swarming with mice begot of the mud of Nilus' was offered as explanation of a plague of rodents to a European traveller in Cairo during the sixteenth century.

The ancient Egyptians were very well aware of the complex natural rhythms that controlled their existence in the Nile Valley and which, in their daily experience, usually worked in fruitful harmonies. They recognized, therefore, that the drama of the creation and the establishment of the natural order in their environment had been a complex affair. Their speculations on the matter contained both religious and scientific theories all bound together, and the many different solutions they found to their questions were all considered to be equally valid. The ancient Egyptians held no religious texts as law, there were no universal truths that had been revealed to them by a god or by a prophet – their many different accounts of the creation did not cancel each other out. Indeed, the scribes and the artists often deliberately constructed clever combinations of images taken from the many different creation stories. The very complexity of this cross-referencing, it seems, symbolized the mystery of many strange

A colossal statue of Amenhotep III lying half-buried in the silt near
the king's mortuary temple in western Thebes

interlinking events. Inconsistencies in the stories – at one point, for example, the formless and surfaceless waters suddenly find shape enough to admit the appearance of the primeval mound – certainly caused few problems to the Egyptians, and they made little effort to explain away such stumbling blocks which, to us, might seem significant contradictions.

No abstract speculations about the creation of their world have survived from ancient Egypt and, indeed, if they had, they would have been expressed in that marvellously concrete pictorial writing – hieroglyphs. Unlike the abstract symbols that form the letters of our Latin alphabet, these Egyptian signs always remained recognizable as independent images, symbols of tangible things. Connections between the images of the hieroglyphs and the meanings of the words that, in combinations, they spelled and signified were considered to be real and significant. This simple process of double meanings, which might seem to us to be little more than a game, held further proofs for the ancient Egyptians of the profound underlying unity shared by the apparently disparate elements of their world. To describe and to understand such underlying designs in the universe, to recognize its unity, is, surely, an objective of most religions.

So, the many stories of the creation did not contradict but complemented each other to become an expression of the awe with which the people regarded the unity that they perceived in their environment.

Such an explanation of the function of these multitudes of ancient myths does not, of course, come from the people themselves – it is a modern analysis of what the surviving fragments of evidence might mean. It is an interesting fact that the long stories about the lives and loves of the Egyptian gods which decorate so many of the older books that describe the ancient faith hardly ever appear as similarly consistent narratives in the ancient texts themselves. These are tales that were first collected by Greek and Roman scholars who were themselves struggling to make some sense of the vast repertoire of ancient signs and snatches of myths which they encountered on their visits to Egypt. Even to a quite untrained eye it is obvious that the ancient religion of Egypt employed a vigorously applied symbolism. During the last century all these ancient signs and symbols were catalogued – like 'flags of the nations' in encyclopedias or the alphabetic lists of telephone directories. But despite this cataloguing, the *faith* that these signs and symbols decorated and which was such a spur to the artists and architects of the ancient nation remained a mystery. Was it really possible that a collection of unlikely yarns and weird signs was the mainspring of a society that was obviously deeply religious and was peopled by a stubborn race of great character? It was about as convincing an explanation of the ancient faith as the glimpses of it that are to be found in the Old Testament.

The Eye of Horus – one of the best known of the ancient symbols – for example, occurs in several of the involved stories about the gods and is

usually associated with aspects of revenge and filial devotion. As a popular
symbol of its day, Horus' Eye was commonly worn as jewellery by the
living and dead alike. It contained many of the same associations that
Christians might feel in connection with the sign of the cross; an unfathomable mix of personal and social images, and emotions. Such symbols hold far more in them than the explanations of storytellers – they hold
the roots of the faith.

The ancient creation myths dealt with the founding of families of gods
that embodied and controlled the elements of the world. One myth, set on
the primeval mound, tells of a creator god, Atum, engendering the first
two gods of the universe by an act of masturbation – a somewhat rustic
solution to the thorny problem of spontaneous generation. Atum's seed
thus produced, made the gods Shu (the atmosphere) and Shu's wife,

The Eye of Horus scratched onto the cliffs of the Valley of the Kings
by an ancient scribe

Tefnut (the water). This couple then begat Geb (the earth) and Nut (the sky). In ancient pictures of this elemental family, Shu is often shown with his arms raised holding his children, the earth and the sky, apart. The first drop of Atum's sperm had not, however, made a god on its appearance, but had fallen into the primeval water to be transformed into hard stone – a steep sided pyramidion whose form was later used in the great temples, topping the shafts of the huge stone obelisks. These pyramidions were sheathed with gold, the very skin of the gods.

As well as these most basic elements, the sun also first appeared on the primeval hill. One story tells that it broke from a large egg that had been left on the mound by a creator god. Eggs, of course, also contain birds and this one was no exception: from it emerged the first goose to fly honking away; and this was the utterance of the first sounds. Another version of the sun's birth tells of it rising from the centre of the petals of a flowering lotus that was floating on the formless waters. When the sun first appeared high in the sky it established itself at the apex of the pyramidion – like a sculpture on a base.

There were other creation dramas in which the creator gods spoke words which simply brought into being objects as they were named. Words of different meanings but having similar sounds also created each other in connecting chains in a manner similar to the mysterious link between hieroglyphic image and meaning. Thus the tears, *remyt*, of the creator god made men, *remet*; the saliva, *netit*, of the creator god made the gods themselves, *neteru*. The words that enjoyed such magical connections appear to have been used almost as a celebration of the power and mystery of the process of writing, where thoughts were captured in lines and images.

As a child of the gods, the king of Egypt became one with them on his death and so the royal tomb was also identified with the mound of creation. For as the sun god and the other deities of the Egyptian universe were joined to the identity of the king so the processes of creation were also, of necessity, joined to those of royal resurrection. Both, after all, required a basic generative force and without this Egypt would have been helpless: the sun would have died, the river would not have flooded and the crops would not have sprouted.

Such extraordinary multiplications of ideas, such labyrinthine inter-twinings of image and meaning held, for the ancient Egyptians, the real truth; a truth which they expressed with tremendous force in the huge monuments they raised for the royal dead. The pyramids, one of the forms of the royal tombs, were the nuclear reactors of ancient Egypt: the throne of the sun itself.

But the colossal scale of the pyramids was never necessary for the expression of ancient Egyptian belief. One of the most extraordinary qualities of their sculpture is exactly this ability to effect an incredible

Geb, the earth god, with Amun's goose standing on his head ; from a scene in the burial chamber of the tomb of Ramesses IX in the Valley of the Kings

Sunset in the city of Thebes; the view from the First Pylon of the Temple of Karnak

change of scale, from the largest statues ever made to statuettes so small that a magnifying glass is necessary to see their details. One description of the mechanism of the sunrise, for example, revolved around a humble scarab beetle who tirelessly rolled a small ball of animal dung (which in reality housed the beetle's larvae and was buried by the insect in the desert sand) from within the sand of the eastern desert and onto the horizon every morning. Thus, the ball of dung became the sun and the little scarab beetle, by its constant effort, was seen to have propelled the resurrected sun to the horizon every dawning. Carvings of the busy little insect were very popular amulets and represented, among other things, notions of 'becoming' or 'potential'.

All the gods of ancient Egypt, of which there are large numbers, fit into two basic categories. First, there is a three-tiered hierarchy, at the top of which are the creator gods, the personifications of the basic elements of the world, and the elders of the creation myths such as Nut and Atum. None of these were worshipped nor did they have their own cults or temples. However, their children and grandchildren – the second level of this hierarchy, consisting of gods like Isis and Osiris – directly affected the prosperity of Egypt in many diverse ways; they had temples and were objects of popular devotion throughout the land. Different families of these gods were associated with different towns and regions of the country. At the third level were more minor gods who directly affected the stuff of daily life: childbirth, travel, the home etc., and who were revered everywhere in the country by the ordinary people, who sometimes maintained small shrines for them in their homes.

This horizontal stratification may be divided vertically into the second of our basic categories: those connected with the solar gods, like Re and Horus, who moved in daily cycles across the sky, and those connected with the annual processes of fertility such as Osiris, and his brother, Seth.

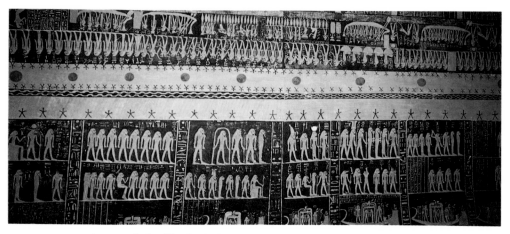

Astronomical ceiling in the burial chamber of the tomb of Ramesses VI
in the Valley of the Kings

Locking the system together was a web of complex familial relationships. Horus, for example, was, in another of his identities, the son of Osiris and when this Horus, the king of Egypt, died, he became his father and in death, fertilized his wife/mother to thus engender his own rebirth!

Such multiple images are found throughout all aspects of the religion. So, as the royal tomb was, in one of its identities, the primeval mound of creation, so each separate royal tomb became a separate creation mound. The temples of Egypt also held primeval mounds which were sometimes represented in the form of the bases on which stood the figures of the gods. One of the greatest of the New Kingdom kings, Seti I, realized many of these complex images in concrete form in an extraordinary building that he had erected at Abydos – one of the great religious centres of Egypt, where Osiris, the fertility god who protected and educated the people of Egypt, had a grave.

In some ways, Seti I's strange temple was shaped like a royal tomb; it was cut deep into the limestone that underlies the loose desert sands that lie behind the cultivated fields of the valley. The main hall of this subterranean building was approached from a downward sloping tunnel whose long walls were covered in the splendid royal funerary texts of the period. Down the full length of the great hall ran two rows of ponderous granite pillars, and at the room's centre was a primeval mound made of the same stone – the stage for the resurrection of the king. At the time of the inundation the great hall flooded and the stone mound was surrounded by the fertilizing waters which held the generative powers of Osiris himself. Judging by the elaborate mortuary texts in the temple it is apparent that the mound was intended to hold the royal spirit after the king's death and to enable it to receive the special benefits of the regenerative power of Osiris, benefits exemplified by the rising waters of the Nile. Around this underground cenotaph was a grove of the sacred persea tree, which stood

31

in specially dug pits of soil placed in the near-white desert sand. The building was a wonder that was still visited and marvelled at by ancient Greek tourists a thousand years after Seti's death.

Many of the temples had pools of primeval water in their enclosures: lakes that were used for both ritual and for practical purposes. The huge rectangular lake by the side of the temple of Amun-Re at Karnak had elaborate sandstone slides running down into it so that the sacred geese of the god, descendents of the goose that had laid the egg of the sun, could waddle from the sacred fowl yards where they lived and swim on the sacred waters.

The sacred lakes were also an indispensable element in the ritual life of the temple. The priests ritually washed in their waters to cleanse themselves for their duties in the house of the god – the temples' innermost sanctuaries, where the sacred figures stood on their primeval mounds. Inside the temples, the priests conducted their ceremonies in the name of the king, opening the doors of the god's shrines in which were the figures of the gods. Every sunrise the seals that closed the shrines were broken and the ritual acts of cleansing, fumigation, offering, and worship were performed. Every evening, after further rituals, the gods were sealed into their sanctuaries for the night. While these rituals were performed in concert with the rising and the setting of the sun, other larger and more elaborate events took place around the temple's yearly calendar.

The temple rituals held echo upon echo of different mythic events. Their richness and complexity was so intense that not one part, however obscure or unintelligible, could be ignored by the participants for fear of spoiling the thread of the great weave of myths. 'Doing the right thing'

The Osireon in the desert at Abydos. The Primeval Hill in the centre of the great hall is covered with water

32

was essential for world order; ritual was far more important than dogma, which hardly existed as a coherent subject. And, as all the elements of their society were woven into the multiplicity of cross references, so the pictorial language that expressed it was amazingly subtle. Many of the individual symbols were a part of daily life and as such we can hardly respond to them in the same instinctive way. Nor can we ever truly penetrate the ancient wisdom in terms of its cult, its magic, or its effect. We are left, therefore, with the simple ability to understand it as a system of thought that was, on its own terms, logical and, if we are prepared to admit to its deep seriousness, capable of penetration by modern minds.

Here is a contemporary account of the ancient faith in action. It is a description, translated from the hieroglyphs of a large granite stela, of a visit by Pianky, a king of the Twenty-fifth Dynasty to the principal temple of the sun god Re at Heliopolis, now part of a modern suburb of Cairo. Pianky, a Nubian king, was in the process of conquering Egypt and he stopped at the great temple of the sun god to perform the royal rituals which would confirm him as king of Egypt and, thus, his opponents as rebels against all established order. Political and religious activities are here all bound into one.

Before entering the temple Pianky ritually cleansed himself in the temple's sacred lake:

His purification was performed, and he was cleansed in the pool, he bathed his face in the river of Nun [the waters of chaos], in which Re bathes his face. Proceeding to the sand hill in Heliopolis [this was a creation mound – Osiris' tomb at Abydos was sometimes called 'the second Heliopolis'] a great oblation was made in the presence of Re at his rising, consisting of white oxen, milk, myrrh, incense and every sweet-smelling wood. He came, proceeding to the House of Re, and entered into the temple with great praise. The chief ritual priest praised the god that the rebels might be repelled from the king. The enrobing chamber was visited that the ritual sedeb-garment might be fastened on; he was purified with incense and libations; garlands for the pyramidion house [in this temple, untypically, the figure of the god stood on a stone pyramidion] were presented to him and flowers were brought to him. He ascended the steps to behold Re in the pyramidion house. The king himself stood alone, he broke through the seals on the bolts, opened the double doors and beheld his father Re in the glorious pyramidion house, the Morning-Bark of Re, and the Evening-Bark of Re [the sun god crossed the sky in a great bark – an obvious way of travelling long distances in the Nile Valley!] He closed the double doors, applied the clay and sealed them with the king's own seal. He charged the priests: 'I have proved the seal; none other shall enter therein of all the kings [rebels] who arise'. The priests threw themselves upon their bellies before his majesty, saying 'To abide, to endure without perishing, O Horus, beloved of Heliopolis'.

33

CHAPTER THREE
COUNTRY LIFE

Today we are hardly inclined to accept the ancient Egyptian accounts of how that country came into being as satisfactory. We want explanations that ring true to our own experience and, unlike the ancient Egyptians, our experiences are of societies that consciously and aggressively undergo a virtually continuous transformation. Periods of ancient history that especially excite our interest are, therefore, those that share some of these attributes, even though they may not be typical of the culture and were of small importance to the ancient people themselves, who valued permanence and stability. Beginnings are of special interest for us: they are the foundations on which all later enterprise is built, the key, perhaps, to our understanding of the ancients. Unfortunately, this search for the origins of things sometimes has us looking hard at the conjuror's hat rather than at the rabbit he has pulled out of it.

Many of the historians, who described the emergence of the culture of ancient Egypt as coming 'out of the mud' of its prehistory (as they somewhat graphically put it), discussed the theories of other scholars more than the ambiguous remnants that show the transformations of the ancient society. This is understandable, for accounts of a rise to power and riches, of the 'advance' of a 'primitive' predynastic people towards the noble simplicities of the Old Kingdom can, consciously or unconsciously, point a moral finger to the paths modern society should take – suggesting remedies for our ills that have been 'proven' by tradition and ancient success. It is a point of view that not only requires a great deal of hindsight but also enough self-confidence to imagine that, at last, the driving force, the destiny of the human race has been understood!

The notion that human societies grow and die like plants was, and indeed still is, a common one and many have tried to explain the mechanisms by which such a dramatic process could operate. In fact, it is simply a biological metaphor for change that is partly derived from the theory of

The Landscape of Nagada. The ancient cemetery was situated between the two low ridges that lie in the haze of the desert's edge, beyond the cultivated fields

evolution and partly from certain widely held beliefs of the past two centuries. Initially, Darwin's theory was seen as a threat to Christianity and the established order but it was soon transmogrified to become a union between biological and social change which, in its turn, came to be equated with native intelligence and moral development! But, in reality, there has never been any evidence to suggest that the predynastic people of Egypt were any more or less moral or intelligent than their successors or, for that matter, than us.

The remnants of the beginnings of ancient Egyptian culture were first encountered in sufficient amounts to allow for their understanding in a remote part of the Nile Valley close to the interface of the fields and the desert strip that runs to the foot of the Valley's cliffs. Inadvertantly, the nearby town of Nagada, locally famed for its bright woven cloths and a particularly potent distillation of dates, has given its name to one of the most pregnant periods of ancient Egyptian history.

Apart from a seemingly endless row of electric pylons that run through the site carrying the power generated at the Aswan Dam to the north, the ancient town site is as bare today as it has been for the past 5,000 years when the Nile, moving eastwards in its bed across the green valley, left it high and dry. Even before the river changed its course the cemetery of the ancient town was situated in the arid, elevated gravel banks of a dry wash, a strange natural landscape of horizontals and symmetrically opposed slopes of almost architectural clarity and regularity.

In the rare event of flash flood following a storm on the desert plateau above, the fast moving waters would pour off the cliffs and tear down through the wash to flood the fields below. Such destructive floods, which still occur almost every year somewhere in the Nile Valley, were more common during the fifth millenium B.C., when the high desert was not as dry as it is now. At that time the desert rainfall may even have been sufficient to allow the inhabitants of the Valley to graze cattle and sheep on sparse winter vegetation. Small mobile groups had harvested wild wheat for many thousands of years but they had never planted seed or settled into fixed communities. Perhaps, because of the comparative ease of their lives, the Nile dwellers did not need to change their ways until much later than their Near Eastern neighbours. For, although it is certain that they profited from some of the innovations of their agrarian neighbours in Anatolia and Iraq there is no hard evidence for the existence of settled villages and towns in the Nile Valley until the beginning of the fourth millenium B.C.

The enormous ancient cemetery at Nagada, which remains to this day the most important site of these farming communities, was discovered in 1895 by Sir Flinders Petrie − a truly remarkable individual then at the height of his extraordinary career. Employing Edward Cecil's description of Kitchener, a colleague of Petrie's said of him that once he had set

The predynastic cemetery at Nagada, opened by Petrie in 1895

himself a job everything else – 'comforts, affections, personalities, were all quite inferior considerations . . . He felt he was defrauding the Almighty if he did not carry out the task'. On Petrie's excavations his co-workers suffered discomforts that have since become legends of archeology. He once claimed: 'I regard the saving of sixpence as a sacred duty'; although even he complained that one year, owing to a constant feeling of nausea, he had become so thin that his skin 'hung on my bones like an old cloak'. His annual recovery from such archeological indispositions, he calculated, had cost him one month each year and it was 'a considerable drain on working time'. One wonders why he did not invent penicillin to cope with the situation!

A scathing critic of lesser mortals – he once described a major French excavation as a 'piteous ruin' – Petrie was himself a brilliant intuitive field worker, a born archeologist if there ever was one. Many of his hurried but remarkably informative reports of his work – often performed in appalling conditions with all sorts of extra-archeological difficulties – are still the only original sources of information on many egyptological questions. When he died in 1942 Petrie had excavated for nearly sixty years and published a thousand books and articles, all stamped with his most

37

distinctive personality. At Nagada, by a peculiarly symbiotic process, not uncommon in archeology, Petrie has become a part of the ancient site so that today it is virtually impossible to discuss the prehistoric people without also coming into contact with the mind of the archeologist who so painstakingly disinterred them.

Petrie's attention had first been drawn to Nagada during a walking survey of a fifty-mile strip of the desert edge, when pottery from the cemetery had been shown to his expedition by the inhabitants of the nearby village of Tukh. In the previous year he had excavated the temples buried in the town of Kuft across the river from Nagada in the hope of finding the remains of the ancestors of the ancient Egyptians who, Petrie believed, had entered Egypt, after a boat journey from Mesopotamia, by a desert wadi that joined the Nile Valley at that town. At Kuft he had found spectacular evidence for this theory, and while there he began training his workforce into the highly skilled excavation team whose descendants still work for archeologists in Egypt.

It was fortunate that Petrie discovered the immense ancient cemetery for, although he did not immediately recognize the true age and significance of the large quantity of grave goods, his team – so ably trained by him – dug the site with a care that by contemporary standards was elaborate and painstaking.

During the three months at the site, Petrie and his men cleared almost three thousand graves. 'The pottery increased so that we soon had to turn it out of the courtyard [of the expedition house], excepting the rarest and

De Morgan's reconstruction of the huge brick tomb that he discovered close to Petrie's cemetery at Nagada. It measures some 27m along its shorter sides

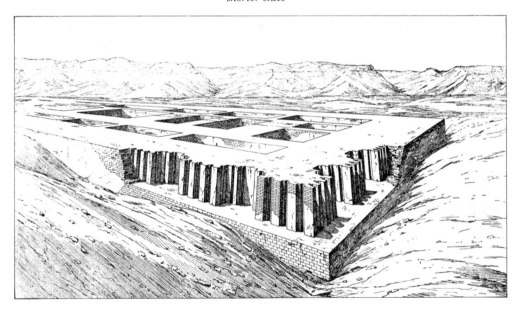

finest vases: and a field of stacked pottery occupied all the space far out in front of the premises. The bones were stacked up in the courtyard until we could scarcely get out of our huts, and inside my hut the more perishable and valuable things filled all the spare space – under my bed, on shelves, and in heaps.' In vain the excavators looked for evidence that would indicate the age of the burials that they were uncovering. It was not for another two years, when the French archeologist Jacques de Morgan discovered a royal tomb nearby that contained examples of similar grave goods, that they were able to ascribe the tombs to a specific age. The tomb, a vast rectangle whose longer sides measured more than 150 feet constructed of elaborately bonded mud bricks, had been built, according to hieroglyphic inscriptions on the grave goods, at the beginning of the First Dynasty. It also contained pottery similar to that which Petrie had found in burials that were, apparently, of the last phases of the Nagada cemetery. The cemetery, then, was predynastic – the first to be identified from that remote era and it held graves that were so large and so well stocked they probably held some of the members of the ruling family. Unlike those of the later dynastic culture, some of the largest and most impressive burials were of women.

But what were the temporal relationships between the separate burials in the Nagada cemetery? Petrie had long been a convinced believer in the 'rise and fall' theory of civilizations being expressed by the design of even its humblest products, and among the grave goods he perceived many indications of this process. Interestingly, it was at about the same time that German excavators working in Greece, following the work of a brilliant group of art historians, chiefly their fellow countrymen, had begun to classify groups of objects in sequences dictated by the birth and decay of their stylistic features. But Petrie took this process a stage further. He classified *all* the Nagada pottery – which included material that in the most part would have been discarded by his contemporaries – into nine main types using shape and ceramic composition as his criteria. He gave this artefact corpus, which also included sub-varieties, distinguishing letters, and then each tomb and its contents was listed on a separate slip of paper. One slip might read: (Tomb number) 3; (Pottery Types) B53, P11, F31, W19, R21, 17, etc.; these items were followed by notes on the rest of the tomb's contents. Clearly, if Petrie's pottery classification reflected a developmental change it would be possible to correlate the individual burial groups and construct an overall sequence of the interments. Though Petrie was not able to establish a sequence of fixed dates by this method, he was able to describe accurately the transitions of the culture that he had found. Today such an analysis would be an obvious candidate for the attentions of a computer programmer but in 1899 Petrie used slips of paper $\frac{1}{4}$ inch wide and 7 inches long which he ruled into nine columns – one for each of his basic pottery types.

Petrie's classification not only brought order to his Nagada material but it was also later used to great effect by archeologists excavating other predynastic sites. In a short while the Sequence Dating System (as Petrie called it) was vindicated when pottery was found in successive strata at several excavations that showed the same developments. It was later extended by finds in other excavations, and it has since been established that the dates of the System overlap the beginnings of dynastic culture. To this day it remains egyptology's sole contribution to archeological method. But it was an invention not always appreciated by his contemporaries, one of whom wrote: 'We cannot pretend to reconstitute history with potsherds only . . . Local taste, local fashion are the only laws which [the potter] obeys, and any sequence or development of forms, arranged in chronological order, is quite out of the question'.

But, happily, the Nagada potters *had* unconsciously followed specific sequences of design in their work, a fact that Petrie had intuitively grasped and used as the basis for his analysis. Subsequent work has shown that his original scheme is often inaccurate and, today, Petrie must be corrected. However, the dialogue of this reform uses Petrie's terminology and aims only to modify his basic system.

Like many Englishmen of his day Petrie had scant respect for the French, especially those who, like de Morgan, directed the Antiquities Department of the Egyptian Government and thus controlled the activities of the foreign archeologists, including Petrie. Nevertheless, Petrie always recognized that it had been de Morgan – himself a distinguished prehistorian – who discovered and established the era of the huge cemetery. Petrie later claimed that de Morgan was actually 'the son of Jack Morgan, a Welsh mining engineer'.

According to modern estimates, the burials at the Nagada cemetery had been made over a period of some fifteen hundred years, the last having been interred around 3050 B.C. The graves were cut into the sandy gravels of the wash in variously shaped pits which, today, pock the silent landscape like the shell holes of an old battlefield. The bodies in the graves were of all ages and both sexes. Most were folded into the so-called foetal position, like unborn babies in their mother's wombs. Apart from the large numbers of pots that lay by the bodies in regularly recurring patterns that suggest a ritual significance, there were hosts of other objects that Petrie also accommodated in his Sequence Dating System. There were decorative slates on which cosmetics had been ground – decoration of the body was widely used by many early races – as well as much other equipment of predynastic daily life: fish hooks, mace heads, large elegant hair ornaments of bone, bracelets, flint tools and weapons. Some of the latter were beautifully worked; first by careful grinding to make the shape, then by gently flaking away the flat surface to produce the characteristic ripple of such weapons and tools. In section they are similar to an aerofoil and they

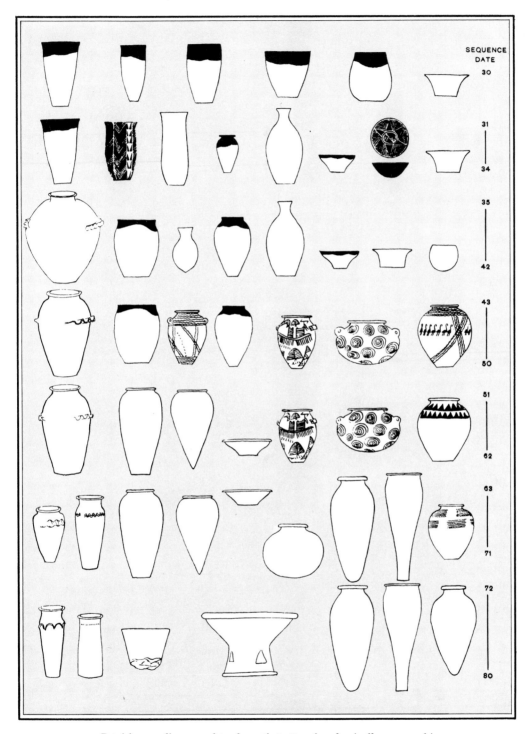

SEQUENCE
DATE
30
31
34
35
42
43
50
51
62
63
71
72
80

Petrie's own diagram of predynastic pottery 'mechanically arranged in its main outlines by various tests'. This, his Sequence Dating System, was first published in 1901

represent the apotheosis of this most ancient art. In addition to the pottery there were other ceramics, and all had been built up without the aid of a potter's wheel, superbly formed and of the most sensitive craftsmanship. Even before he could date his discoveries Petrie was never in any doubt that he had excavated the memorials of a vigorous and most talented culture; the small fragments that still litter the site show this same superb quality. Much of the fine burial pottery of Nagada is as different from utilitarian wares as a green celadon bowl is from a plastic plate. The potters at the ancient town had elevated their craft to an art and it was never equalled by any of the later potters of Egypt.

The cemetery tells us much about ancient care and excellence. And in the ordering and quality of its grave goods it displays the tender pre-occupation the living had with the dead, and their belief in the necessity

A predynastic grave excavated in 1908 by two of Petrie's ex-pupils at El Mahasna, a site close to Nagada. The body – that of woman – had originally been wrapped in a reed mat. Two slate palettes, used for grinding green malachite eye paint, lie near her hands. These, and the pottery above her head, date the burial, numbered H 22 by its excavators, as 'Late Nagada II' (at latest about 3100 B.C.)

of their continued well being – traits that were also typical of the Dynastic Civilization that followed.

The town that filled this cemetery lies in an area that is now half culti-vated and half desert. On the desert edge Petrie excavated a part of the ancient settlement and found the remains of buildings made of sun-dried mud brick. Most of the ancient town, however, remains unexcavated, waiting for the attentions of archeologists who, during the late 1970s, have started to work at Nagada again. Very little is known about this predynastic culture and what we do know has come almost exclusively from cemeteries, several more of which have been discovered since Petrie's work at Nagada. That the towns remain largely unexcavated is a great pity, for it was in these settlements that an extraordinary social change reached its conclu-sion: the final stages of the transition from peripatetic groups that hunted and gathered wild seeds to settled communities of farmers who planted crops, domesticated animals, and lived in sedentary family units.

It has been estimated that of the time that the human race has existed ninety-five per cent has been spent in groups that hunted and gathered. Agrarianism, which can be traced back in time for thousands of years before the good people of ancient Nagada, must have engendered a com-pletely new set of responses in man to the world in which he now lived. For the first time these settled communities allowed the possibility of specialization of occupations: potters, hunters, farmers, fishermen and, inevitably, organizers and supervisors, rulers and priests. The foundations of human society were laid. In the cemetery of Nagada we can see that during its fifteen hundred years of use there was a process of selection taking place: a choice was being made by the community as to who would be buried in the graveyard and with what standard of grave goods. Some of the later graves were so elaborate in their shape, so richly furnished with grave goods, and so large in their dimensions that Petrie and later scholars have not hesitated to describe them as the tombs of chiefs or kings – the predecessors of Pharaoh.

It could be said that what Petrie found at Nagada were the missing links in the long chain that represented the transformation of Egyptian society, joining small centres of tribal cultures to the basic elements of the Dynastic Civilization. This chain pulled hard and strong throughout the history of ancient Egypt and represents a connection with its past – a connection that in modern societies has long been broken by the adoption of new religions and the introduction of revolutionary technologies. As far as we know, the group of hunters and gatherers that had lived in the Nile Valley before the farming communities had established themselves belonged to the broad pattern of Stone Age culture that ran across Western Asia and into Europe. But once farming communities were established in the closed environment of the Nile Valley their cultures quickly developed distinctive personalities and remained largely independent of major outside influences. And many of the traits and characteristics that were present in the communities of Nagada and its contemporaries remained a part of the unique personality of ancient Egyptian culture until its end.

Despite the revolutions in archeological and historical method that have taken place since Petrie's day – methods that in many cases he invented or pioneered – there is still much about the life of these ancient societies that remains unknown and will always continue to be so. The practical, social, and economic factors that arise in the apparently simple process of hand-making pottery, for example, can still be seen at the potteries of Ballas, a village close to ancient Nagada and just a stone's throw from the royal tomb discovered by de Morgan. Until recently these potteries provided Upper Egypt with the distinctive water pots that village women carry on their heads to and from the river. Nowadays, plastic and tin containers, which are lighter and less vulnerable to damage, are often used instead and the industry is under some pressure. However, the Ballas jars are still common objects in every Upper Egyptian village and may still be bought for the equivalent of thirty pence, or about sixty cents.

The sheer bulk of this industry – for that is what it is – makes the conclusions drawn from a close comparison with the painstaking work of the ancient potters dangerous. Nevertheless, the fact remains that it is the modern aspect of a tradition of potting in the area that has continued for

some 7,000 years. On the ground outside the sheds of the modern potters fragments of the work of their ancient predecessors may still be found. Equally, although the religion and the economy of the potters has changed since the age when Nagada was a centre of the world's cultural development, the present potteries do represent a fine example of how different their processes are from those employed in modern factories. The Ballas potteries engage the greater part of the community in their work, relying heavily on contacts within the family and village circles. Potting remains a village industry whose complexities could hardly be inferred from only studying its sturdy products.

The clay used for most of the Ballas pots comes from the beautiful purple *gebel*, the line of limestone cliffs that the town shares as a common backcloth with the ancient cemetery. Low down in the limestone runs a fifty-metre-broad band of loose clayey shale which, in certain favourable sections, is dug by the villagers and loaded onto camels to be brought to the potters' shed situated on the fringe of the desert behind the town. The small pieces of shale are dumped from the camels' panniers into circular stone-lined pits, and then covered with water that has been hauled from adjoining wells. The shale expands and disintegrates when it is soaked and the next day water buffaloes are set to trample around in circles in the pits to render the lumpy mass into the even, green clay that the potter will work. The process of preparing the clay for use – kneeding and pounding it into suitable balls – is common to all craftsmen potters, but the production of the pots, in two pieces made on separate days in batches of about

Left *Modern water jars stacked at the potteries of Ballas*

Right *A Ballas potter at his wheel. The gentle curve that he has thrown in the soft clay will be enlarged and closed to form the bottom of a water jar*

one hundred, is the work of a few skilled men – the jobbing craftsmen. The two pieces are joined on the wheel and an assistant, usually a young boy, carries the pots on an elegant back-turned wrist, outside the shed to dry in the sun. The boy also replenishes the potter's wheel with fresh clay and ensures that, in the high temperature of the desert, the stocks of clay and half-completed pots are not allowed to dry out before they are finished.

The kilns in which the pots are fired are basically of Roman design. They are fuelled with dried sugarcane leaves and, after three days of cooling, the contents are removed and camels take them to the riverside to be loaded onto boats for distribution throughout the Nile Valley. There is a high rate of spoilage: fired but imperfect pots are valued locally for building materials and a great part of the local villages are made, picturesquely enough, from the spoiled pots. Ever practical, Petrie's publication of the ancient cemetery includes an account of his team's accommodation and outlines the methods its members used to build their expedition houses from the damaged vessels!

The pots made from the shale are a dull white with a greenish-beige tint; the red pottery, also produced at Ballas, is not made from the shale but from a mixture of dung ash (from the cooking fuel used in the village hearths) and Nile silt dug from the fields and carefully sieved. This dull red ware is used for a wide variety of purposes, including charcoal braziers, many different cooking implements, and even stools. As well as the traditional water pots a white ware is used for water storage and as drinking-water containers. Although the same vessels have been made for centuries, each potter can tell the work of his colleagues. Potteries in other nearby towns make their own individual pottery shapes from the distinctive local clays. The whole area, indeed, has long been renowned for these products and the practical Arab travellers who visited Upper Egypt in the Middle Ages – the first chroniclers of the region since Roman times – have more to say about these wares than they do about the ancient monuments that are such a dramatic feature of the local landscape.

Economically, the pottery has provided the village with an income additional to the one usually obtained in Upper Egypt from tilling the soil. Perhaps it is this that gives the villagers such a strong sense of local identity and self-assurance. The potteries operate during the agriculturally unproductive months of spring and early summer, before the time of harvest when, in any case, high temperatures and excessive dryness render potting impractical. All the complexity of the village social life is mirrored in its potteries. No one man controls the total process: some people own the camels and employ miners to quarry the shale, while others own the potters' sheds, organize the manufacture of the pots, and hire the potter, who is employed by the kiln-load. The organization of loading and firing the kilns is equally complex. The richest men in the village, I have been told, are those who own the water buffaloes that trample the saturated shale.

And after this extraordinary process of manufacture, all with labour and materials derived from the village and its surroundings, all that archeologists will find, perhaps hundreds of miles away, is just a simple pot or, even, merely a fragment.

Presently, an international group of egyptologists is attempting to establish similar facts about the productions and distribution of the ancient potters. Their pots will be drawn and photographed, charts will standardize descriptions of the colour of their ware and a scientific terminology will describe both their shape and quality. With an accurate sectional drawing and a brief technical text of each pottery type, a complete catalogue of all the surviving work of the ancient potters will have been compiled. All that egyptologists in the future will have to do in order to record their discoveries of ancient ceramics is to list the catalogue numbers that describe the equivalents of the pots that they have excavated. Anthropologists, economists and workers in similar fields will then have an enormous fund of basic information at their fingertips and their studies in such diverse subjects as art history, ancient trading patterns and chronology will be greatly aided.

And at the warm and empty cemetery of Nagada the fragments of the ancient pottery that lie upon the loose gravel beds still show the marks of the craftsman's hands as he worked; some, even, bear his fingerprints, the marks of ancient gestures that instantly close the gap between past and present. Ancient Egypt is still held in the modern Nile Valley. There, in the silence of its ruined monuments, it is contained in qualities that the ancient people recognized and understood, a direct and human bond.

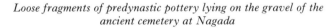

Loose fragments of predynastic pottery lying on the gravel of the ancient cemetery at Nagada

CHAPTER FOUR
MILESTONES

At Abydos in Upper Egypt there are remains dating from nearly all periods of ancient Egyptian history, from the traces of predynastic settlements to the huge temples of the New Kingdom. The site was one of the most sacred in Egypt, where the souls of the dead came from all over the country to gather at a tomb of Osiris. The most popular route of the pilgrim dead was to travel to Abydos by river, and paintings in the ancient tomb chapels show these dead souls embarking for Abydos and returning from their mystic voyage. The endless model boats that are exhibited in the museums of the world are another product of this most practical religion.

The great god's grave was identified by the ancient Egyptians as being the simple mud brick tombs of the First Dynasty kings that lay on a mound in the plain behind the ancient town. These most ancient tombs have been piled so high with the offering pots of later worshippers that they appear as a dull red stain on the light desert sand that surrounds them. Of the ancient town of Abydos there is very little left. The principal object of tourist visits is the famous temple of Seti I – its disconcerting modern exterior belying the beautiful halls and decorations that stand in the darkness beyond the concrete façade. Other temples, their brittle lime-stone walls now largely rendered into builder's quicklime in Roman kilns, lie in tantalizing ruins all around. Old blocks of stone perfectly preserved and bright with ancient painting, appear in enigmatic isolation through the sand. It takes about half an hour to walk from these temples and the nearby ancient town, now a series of holes filled with dank water, to the grave of Osiris. Today the mound is called the Umm el Ga'ab (the Mother of Pots) by the local villagers who seldom venture into the desert beyond their fields.

To reach the Mother of Pots you must pass through a huge cemetery struggling across ridges of small sand dunes which hold the sun and reflect it into your face. In summer it is very hot – sand temperatures have

Small pots that once held offerings which were left at the grave of
Osiris at Abydos now litter the sand of the Umm el Ga'ab

been recorded here of 200°F – and you can become dizzy during the short walk. There is no shade.

The dunes cover desert gravel that was thrown up during the excavation of the cemetery and their sand is still spiced with ancient fragments: potsherds blasted by windblown sand into shiny sharp shapes that resemble half-melted sheets of ice, and wood that glistens strangely and is feather-light, quite desiccated. Abydos is awkward, hot, inconvenient and largely featureless, yet it is a spiritual centre of the ancient people. To walk through it is to walk through an old landscape, part of the universe of the ancient culture.

In 1980 the German Archeological Institute was excavating at the Umm el Ga'ab once again, uncovering the site where, during 1899–1901, Petrie had made the excavations that resulted in the discovery of sufficient inscribed fragments from the royal tombs to enable scholars to reconstruct the chronology of the kings of the First and Second Dynasties. These fragments were gathered together by Petrie from the wrecked tombs which, it had been imagined previously, had been plundered, smashed and excavated beyond all usefulness. Now, in their new excavations, the German archeologists will retrieve further information from the ancient site.

Numerous archeological reports describe the masses of objects that have been taken from Abydos. The fabulous stratified townsite, the rich desert burials, the splendid mature temples like overblown roses – all have been listed, sifted and, in great part, lifted. Nowadays the spirits of the ancient dead return to a dug-over desert plain as choppy as a rough sea. Some twenty volumes describe the extraordinary discoveries that have been made on the Umm el Ga'ab, but at the site itself there is very little to see. Small loose fragments of the royal burial goods lie in the sand mixed with heaps of the offering pots of the later pilgrims. Usually these mounds are quite deserted, left to the ancient Egyptians. Cameras can hardly record the site; perhaps, in the end, Abydos is only a collection of books, a desert littered with footnotes and fragments of ancient legends, archeology, and religious faith. Some landscapes are not easily seen but you can feel them all around you.

Yet, although the ancient life of Abydos has turned into dust or been deposited in museums, the villagers who live near the ancient site have stories about the monuments that hint at the ancient spirit of the place as indeed do other villagers who inhabit the fringes of ancient Egypt. When the wind howls over the mound of the Umm el Ga'ab there is talk of *afarit* – of bad spirits – that roar in the night. One verse of the ancient *Book of the Dead* describes this roaring wind at Abydos as the noise of the spirits of the dead as they assemble by the temple platform, called the 'Terrace of the Great God', for the great annual procession to Osiris' tomb, or as they come down the strange sand-filled canyon that runs

*The crack in the cliffs at Abydos that holds the singing sand. The
mound in the foreground is a small part of the Umm el Ga'ab*

through the cliffs from the high desert down to the plain of the Umm el
Ga'ab. In 1895 archeologists working in the vicinity were startled to hear
'the sounds of high voices and bugles, and rushing sounds ending in a deep
rumbling' echoing around the high canyon walls – the result, geologists
later explained, of the clean and even-grained aeolian sand gently rolling
down the sloping sides of the canyon in slow waves which produce that
unearthly music – music that is also heard in the Hebrides, on the sands
of Eigg.

◆ ● ◆ ●

During the past fifty years ancient Egypt has become a commodity, a
phenomenon subjected to all the pressures of modern sales techniques, its
products displayed like wares in a jewellery shop. And in the process
several alternative interpretations of the ancient civilization have become
elements in the popular consciousness of history, a part of Our Western
Heritage. Carefully nurtured, the evidence of the past has been used to
supply all manner of pedigrees – 'proofs' – for diverse opinions and beliefs.
In this context, the remains of ancient Egypt serve as mirrors of our
modern thought – also, therefore, of our modern society – and, for better or
worse, the specialists we have appointed to be the guardians of our past
are also subject to the myths, fads and pressures of our own time. Their

learned interpretations are sieved through a second skein before they arrive on the doorstep of the public. The first sieve, of course, has been time itself and the arbitary nature of what it has allowed to survive.

From the frequent ambiguities of the evidence of excavation and other scientific researches one moves quickly into the slippery areas of theory and counter-theory and, in this respect, the transformations that occurred at the ending of the predynastic period have been a particularly happy hunting ground for historical hypotheses. Petrie believed that the impetus towards nationhood and the creation of the national culture that took place at that time was provided by a foreign race that invaded Egypt from several routes, principally from the desert *wadi* that runs from Kuft to the Red Sea. This 'Dynastic Race' it was widely believed, became a superior caste that ruled over the weaker settled inhabitants of Egypt and created a Dynastic Civilization. Skull measurements taken from burials in cemeteries such as Nagada were separated into two types: 'advanced invaders' and the 'indigenous proletariat'. The colonizing activities of the Europeans provided the egyptologists with a convincing modern parallel for this version of events, and science in the shape of anthropometry lent a rosy glow of reality to the thesis. Modern-day anthropologists greatly bemoan this obsession with skull measuring at the expense of studying the other numerous human remains, for much information about diet, health and other areas of human activity has been irrevocably lost.

Today the Dynastic Race ('advanced invaders') and the related theories of major external intervention in the creation of ancient Egyptian culture have little to commend them. While it is true that there are many examples of foreign influence in early dynastic culture of Egypt – mainly from the area now called Iraq – these were either discarded or transformed into typically Egyptian forms of expression by the time of the Old Kingdom. It should also be observed that whoever borrows such importations to advance their culture has of necessity, already arrived at the stage when such boons may usefully be employed! Theories of outside influences creating the Egyptian state merely presuppose the mechanisms that they attempt to describe. It simply moves the miracle to Mesopotamia. The main spur of the Dynastic Race theory and the linking notions of radical foreign influence on the Nile dwellers was the conviction that ancient Egypt, an obvious source of European civilization, was 'Mediterranean' and could not have had 'African' origins. Such fearful preoccupations now seem quite beyond the point: the proponents of the Dynastic Race theory would, for example, have a fine old time excavating in a London cemetery attempting to link skull size to the 'national genius'.

Anthropologists have long recognized that the division of the human race into such idealized types is of little use, for these groupings have never provided the basis of cultures or civilizations. In the Nile Valley, the broad spectrum of physical type that has always existed there changes continuously along its banks from the Mediterranean to Central Africa. Attempts to locate the Dynastic Race as a separate entity is as elusive as is the object of a search among the catalogues of racial types for an 'ancient Egyptian'. Culture, not bloodstock, produced the ancient civilization and the origins of that culture were largely indigenous to the people of the Nile Valley. The predynastic Egyptians, then, were exactly the same people as those who composed the dynastic population; in other words a race just as homogeneous and as individual as the Egyptians of today.

But this still leaves, apparently, the problem of the source of the impetus behind the transformations of the predynastic culture into a nation, a change that is well symbolized in the arts by the abandonment of the fluid simplicities of the Nagada craftsmen and the deliberate adoption of the formal rules of the dynastic arts. The puzzle, however, is largely a creation of modern histories and museum displays, and it dissolves when seen in the perspective of time. On average, the Nagada cemetery saw only two burials a year during the 1,500 years of its use. The grave goods from it represent, in fact, an infinitesimally slow drift of style that could hardly have been discernible in a single generation. But when the separate stages of this slow transition are displayed in the exhibits of a single museum case, or contracted into a few pages of book illustrations (and these generally placed next to pictures of the arts of the first dynasties) they appear to fit into a pattern of development like those of the past few hundred years of European art: 'early' and 'late' Nagada (called Nagada I & II) become ghostly entities in themselves, like early or late Picassos.

In fact, it was exactly during the era of the unification of Egypt, at the end of the predynastic period and during the first two dynasties, that the ancient artists began the process of establishing the style which almost everyone can recognize as ancient Egyptian – a style so compact, so characterful that some odd pieces, though obviously of the highest quality, may not be accurately dated by experts, to within a period of some 2,000 years or so! Yet despite this static style, the inner dynamic was intense enough to allow masterpieces, and most individual ones, to be created from its form at almost every period of its 3,000-year-long history.

This style of the dynastic arts was of far more importance to ancient Egypt than some striking product of a few ateliers of artists and architects that were far removed from the centre of life. The two aspects of the culture of ancient Egypt that were central to its incredible longevity and its intense character were the architectural and the art styles. These were the two hinges on which the door of the state was hung, the philosophic language of the nation. The vital logic of the arts, created in harmony with the written language, which itself was a comparatively minor branch, gave voice to the subtle theology that surrounded the king. So important were the arts to ancient Egyptian culture (and must remain so for our understanding of it, for the arts form a major part of what has survived) that they not only mirrored the developments and changes of the ancient society but were, at times, the very embodiment of them. The arts in ancient Egypt were, then, the principal method of organizing and recording experience. If we look with intelligent eyes at the remains of ancient Egypt we can sometimes see the ancient people thinking.

The period of the unification and the first two dynasties – called the Archaic Period – was the time when the use of traditional media by the Egyptian craftsmen, such as ceramic, bone, and ivory, declined and were replaced with other materials and forms that became the basis of the dynastic arts. It was the time when the human figure was measured and set into the grid that was the foundation of all subsequent representations of the human figure by Egyptian artists. Drawn in accordance with this strict canon, the human body became the central motif of the arts, and the grid that was derived from it was used as the standard measuring system in all types of design, from chairs to pyramids. At the same time the other qualities of the dynastic style – the extreme sensitivity to surface and

The ceremonial palette of King Narmer. The figure of the king, who wears the crown of Upper Egypt, breaks the head of an enemy with a stone mace while other Lower Egyptian town-dwellers flee the conquering king. The overall design of this palette is carefully regulated; the king's triumphal pose is the forerunner of dozens of similar scenes cut into the walls of Egyptian temples over a period of more than three thousand years

outline, the special spatial qualities of drawing and relief – were all being explored, developed and codified.

This was the time, then, when the grammar of the arts – the fixed infra-structure of canon and proportion – was established. Such stern formal rules were essential to communicate the style to succeeding generations, and in a country where both changelessness and exactitude were all, where both priests and artists were the curators of the nation and its culture, such accurate communication from generation to generation was essential.

Typically, the few major works that have survived from this period, the famous palette of Narmer, the stela of Djet-Hor, do not display a struggle for attainment, they do not even betray a careful formal development leading towards the new style and away from the lively informal arts of the Nagada period. They are tensionless, perfect products, and this effortless-ness and apparent passivity is one that, in stone, is very hard bought. It is a quality that is also typical of later work. In the great stone temples of the New Kingdom, the columns stand as if weightless – there is none of the dynamism of the expression of load and support that is central to the European tradition and which was born, of course, in the temples of classical Greece. It is this apparent ease of attainment that at first glance can disappoint the visitor from the West. For, without this visible ex-pression of stress there is, apparently, no sense of the heroic, of national destiny or of fate.

Of all the centres of late predynastic culture that existed in Upper Egypt, one close to Abydos, the town of This, seems to have emerged as the strongest city of the region. From here the armies of the predynastic warlords set out, taking town after town as they moved northwards along the Nile Valley. The names of the leaders and the dates of their campaigns remain unknown, and there are very few records of the battles and nego-tiations that must have taken place. What have survived are fragments reminiscent of mythic epics, like pieces of Greek vases that show the deeds of Achilles, or the journeys of Odysseus.

The ancient Egyptians believed that a king, Menes, had united their land and founded its capital Memphis – the first the world had ever known – in the region between the end of the Nile Valley and the beginning of the Delta. Our western term 'Egypt' (modern Egyptians call their country Misr) is a corruption of that capital's ancient name which embodied the name of its patron deity, a local god called Ptah. It was he who had made the universe – not by participating in a series of rustic incidents but by the act of formulating and naming the elements of the world aloud. It was highly appropriate that the first capital of united Egypt had as its patron this god, who not only embodied the abstract concept of the creation of

Egypt, as did Menes, but was also the patron of artists and craftsmen, professions that were themselves involved in the creation and maintenance of the Egyptian culture.

At first, Memphis was a fortress built by southern kings in a northern province. Doubtless one of its ancient names 'White Walls', described the appearance of this city enclosed within a great rectangle of white-washed mud brick wall built with a distinctive panelled façade that in all probability imitated the appearance of the royal palace, a huge portable pavilion with a great wooden frame hung with matting like a vast beduin tent, a large impressive structure that housed the court and the royal administration as it moved throughout the land. The great rectangular royal palace with its recessed walls and bright hanging carpets symbolized the power and total authority that issued from it. It must have presented a terrifying aspect to the town and village dwellers, whose habitations reflected their agrarian lifestyle, and were controlled by practical considerations and not the rigidly ruled rectangles of the royal edifice.

The predynastic lords had not campaigned across Egypt to return to their southern cities in triumph with their freshly won booty like Romans or Assyrians, but they created a single nation from their conquests. The state they made was one of royal monopolies, taking much of the power of trade and commerce to themselves. There was also a religious monopoly; the king alone met with the gods that governed the nation's natural resources; he built the gods' houses, the great temples of Egypt. The gods of Egypt, and there were many different families of them in the regions of the country, saw to their home provinces. But there was only one force that overlooked the welfare of the entire land: the king. He owed no special allegiance to any part of his country, had no place but the throne and had responsibility for the whole nation. And as the 'royal progress' through Egypt was continuous during the king's lifetime, so after death the king circulated in cosmic harmony with the gods for the benefit of his people. These were the mechanisms on which the religious and social unity of the nation was built. Take away the faith of a religious person and he is left in a random and meaningless world, one empty of effect and purpose: destroy the king of ancient Egypt and the vital link with cosmic order, the fulcrum of the state, was lost.

With such a dramatic gathering together of power about the royal person, the separate cities and provinces that had existed before the unification were profoundly changed. The cities' previous functions, as trading centres, of seats of local control and defence, were no longer relevant and many of them withered away. Archeological investigation of the Delta cities and the colonies of Egyptians in Palestine, show just this contraction of wealth after the unification, when many of their functions had been removed to the office of the king. So unusual, so secure, was this state that the ancient king created, so peculiar was its urban structure that

*A decorative panel – a so-called 'false door' – from the enclosure
wall of the mortuary complex of Senusert I of the Middle Kingdom.
It shows the façade of a royal palace of the type inhabited by the
Archaic kings. The doors at the centre of the design have two bolts;
the palace walls are decorated with the geometric patterns of
ancient textiles*

*The huge mortuary palace of a Second Dynasty king, Khasekehmui,
standing in the desert behind the ancient city of Abydos. It still retains
the 'palace façade' decoration – a series of buttresses running along
some of its walls*

it has been claimed to have been a 'state without cities'. However, some communities, which were not dependent on the normal patterns of commerce and war for their wealth but on the largesse of royal piety, prospered. The foundation of temples and tomb chapels, the accommodation of large numbers of pilgrims at national religious festivals which took place throughout the royal calendar, became some of the economic factors that controlled the fortunes of many of the major cities. Abydos, for example, which was a poorly located city in practical terms, prospered greatly, whereas This, the strategically situated provincial capital, shrank to insignificance. In short, there was a profound cultural and economic change throughout the land.

With the king as the essential link between Egypt and the gods, the assurer of prosperity for his people, the royal death assumed the proportions of a national crisis. No one in Egypt believed in the total annihilation of the person after death. The spirits of the dead, attached to the corpse and the tomb that housed it, looked out from their desert graves back over the land in which they had lived, part of the forces of nature that nourished the land. Continuous contact with the dead was maintained by rituals of offering that were conducted around the tomb. There is evidence of similar but simpler patterns of behaviour during the predynastic period.

The king's grave, the dwelling of the royal spirit that was at one with the gods, obviously had immense significance and an elaborate system of offerings was centred on the royal cult that later became one of the principal arteries of economic life, a part of the system of taxes and government that was, thereby, sanctioned by the ultimate power of religion.

Although the first kings of Egypt had made their capital in the north, graves were built for them in the province of This, at Abydos. Here, many of the kings of the Archaic Period were buried in tombs at the Umm el Ga'ab, the site that, later in ancient Egyptian history, became the focus of the cult of the mysteries of Osiris and a place of pilgrimage for both the living and the dead; a subtle identification of the origins of the royal tombs at the Umm el Ga'ab – the tombs of the kings who unified Egypt – that was not far from the archeological truth of the matter!

Perhaps the modest size of these royal tombs on the Umm el Ga'ab had been dictated by the shortage of space at the site for earlier it had been used as a cemetery for some elaborate predynastic graves. But as well as these tombs – simple rectangular sand-filled structures that covered subterranean burial chambers – the archaic kings also had enormous funerary palaces built close by the ancient town of Abydos. These were vast rectangles built of mud brick and decorated with the same recessed panelling that gave the royal palaces their distinctive form. Very little has ever been found inside these gigantic enclosures, but judging from later custom – and the Egyptians always stood in great reverence of the customs of their own early history – these mortuary palaces probably held the ritual equip-

59

ment necessary for the maintenance of the cult of the dead king. Dozens of the royal retainers were buried around the edge of these huge brick rectangles and sometimes the linear patterns of the rows of modest brick-lined chambers are all that remain to mark the positions of the king's huge funerary palaces. These have either been quarried for their brick or simply recycled by the villagers to be used once again as the fertile soil that they had been before the ancient kings had ordered the black river silt to be fashioned into bricks and carried out onto the desert to make the great temples.

As well as the holy graveyard at Abydos, the kings also built tombs for themselves at Memphis, right along the skyline in front of the setting sun, at the very point where heaven and earth meet: the point of the royal death. In form, these tombs were a combination of the two structures at Abydos, a lavish model of the southern original. And as if to emphasize this connection with the south, the measurements and proportions of these tombs were linked, these correspondences often occurring between tombs that had been built hundreds of years apart. From this high desert cemetery – today called Sakkara after a nearby village – the spirits of the kings could oversee the capital founded and controlled by the kings during their lives.

On their outsides these northern tombs were shaped like the rectangular royal palace, and their burial chambers were like those of the Umm el Ga'ab. Rooms that surrounded the burial chamber were packed with everything the king would need for a most vigorous afterlife. It was a lavish system of provisioning for all eternity that was eventually replaced by the complex institutions of mortuary foundations and the daily ministrations of a staff of priests. During the period they were built and stocked, these large storehouses were almost an index of the wealth and life of Egypt at the time. Today these splendid tombs are invariably found badly plundered; nevertheless the fragments that do remain tell us a great deal. The tombs held weapons, tools, beds, stools and other furniture, even in some cases, lavatories. Food there was in great plenty – and at the Umm el Ga'ab one archeologist reported that the sand for a great distance around was still stained with oils and smelled of fine aromatic balsams. Even now, at Sakkara, beeswax left in the ancient tombs smells gently of its ancient bees. The jars and elegant vessels of stone that held these offerings were some of the finest ever made by man. They display an exquisite sensibility towards their beautiful raw materials; often crystal, slate, breccias, even carnelian and amethyst were used; but the ceramic vessels, though large and sturdy, show a general decline since the days of the painstaking work of the Nagada potters.

During the reigns of the first kings these extraordinary tombs, like archaic supermarkets filled with rooms and chambers, were without entrances or connecting doorways. On the outside the decorative shapes

of the panelled façade alone provided the focus for the ritual activities of
the mortuary cult. Later, one of the recessed niches was made deeper than
the rest and provided a focus for the growing activities of the priest at the
site. In the south, it seems that the ceremonies of the cult were conducted
inside the funerary palaces.

Despite their ruin, a process which has been greatly aided by some of
the archeologists who first uncovered the flimsy remains and subsequently
left them exposed to the elements, it is from these monuments that the best
glimpses of the potential and capabilities of the new nation may be gleaned.
The first typically ancient Egyptian free-standing statue to have survived,
for example, was excavated from the remains of a small chapel that was
attached to one of the Sakkara tombs of the late First Dynasty. It shows a
common pose, one foot forward as if the figure were striding; the toes are
individually described, and carefully observed and made. But the statue
exists only as these two feet on their ancient plinth, which is charred and
warped from an ancient fire. So much of the art of this most fascinating
period is like that: smashed and broken, only hinting at what must have
been a time of intense intellectual effort. It is as if the entire Italian
Renaissance had been destroyed and we had to reconstruct this formative
period of European history from tiny fragments of stone and plaster and
a few scraps of written texts.

The interior of a huge tomb of the First Dynasty king, Djet-Hor, that
stands on the western skyline above ancient Memphis. This ruined
monument is similar to the one that de Morgan discovered close by
Nagada cemetery in Upper Egypt. It is some five thousand years old

CHAPTER FIVE

GIANT STEPS

By the end of the First Dynasty, the desert spur that formed the greater part of the western skyline of Memphis had been quite filled with royal tombs, and the kings of the Second Dynasty started a new royal cemetery half a mile to the south. Here the skyline was less regular and parts of the ridge were buried deep beneath the drifted sand of a great dune. Two kings built their tombs behind this dune and, in turn, they were followed to the area by some of the tombs of the next dynasty. Rather than placing their monuments side by side as their forerunners had done, these kings had their tombs sited behind those of their predecessors, going ever further into the desert in a general retreat from the sharp edge of the Memphis horizon.

It was on this desert plateau that the architects of one Third Dynasty king, Djoser, came slowly to the realization of a new form for the royal tomb: the pyramid; and in this they made an image that dominated the life of the nation for a hundred years. In the century that followed Djoser's death, the Egyptians made pyramids so large that to this day they remain the biggest stone structures in the world. The king's tomb had become the site of a national celebration of the potential and power of the nation's culture, a statement in architectural form of the order that had been created in the land.

Small stone structures had been built since the days of the First Dynasty – usually as parts of other buildings made of mud brick – but Djoser's craftsmen transformed this simple technology, which never seems to have consisted of more than a few hundred roughly dressed stones set into a coarse plaster, and, at the site of the royal tomb, made buildings all of stone. These were bounded by a magnificent stone wall, this a great rectangle decorated with the same pattern as the panelled façades of earlier royal tombs. Djoser's walls were, however, nearly six hundred yards along their longer sides and slightly more than half that distance along their shorter. And, as if to emphasize their continuity with

A full-sized dummy building in the enclosure of the Step Pyramid at Sakkara

the past, the measurements of the great enclosure were one hundred times larger than the façade of de Morgan's royal tomb by Nagada in the south, a tomb which in Djoser's day was some four hundred years old. But there the architectural similarities ended, for neither the Egyptians nor anyone else in the world at that time had seen anything quite like those smooth, shining white stone walls.

If these great walls, their design steeped in the traditions of royal tomb architecture, did not sufficiently emphasize the new-found vigour in the land, then the buildings that rose inside them certainly did. Because the tomb was set back from the Sakkara ridge Djoser's architects had to build high to enable it to regain its position of dominance on the Memphis skyline, and that's exactly what they did. They had started by making the tomb a low square structure of well-finished stone with battered walls some 20 cubits (10.6 m) high that was reminiscent of the superstructures of the royal tombs at the Umm el Ga'ab. On top of this sturdy monument Djoser's workmen first built three smaller similarly shaped structures of stone that rose in a series of equal sized steps. Then, in a final dramatic gesture, as if they were intent on taking the royal tomb up into the sky itself, the entire monument was enlarged at its base, enabling two more steps to be added to its top. In this process of transforming the shape of the royal tomb they had built a pyramid – the Step Pyramid – the first in the world.

Djoser's pyramid seen from the Memphite plain

Many different factors influenced the mechanics of this revolutionary process. For example, the traditional material for a royal tomb, mud brick, would never have been able to withstand the stresses of compression in a building nearly two hundred feet high. Pyramids were born of stone, and virtually in the same breath as stone architecture itself. The new material had given immediate expression to a form that the Egyptians could not previously have realized. The whole architectural tradition had been transcended. By piling form on form the Egyptians had created a shape so dramatic that, in unison with its commanding position at the horizon, had joined heaven to earth, earth to heaven. Djoser's pyramid and the buildings that accompanied it were a philosophical statement, part of the language of a nation that thought and responded to their situation in concrete images. And the pyramid's form so charged this nation that for a hundred years the national life revolved around the royal tomb, reducing many of the cities of Egypt to comparative poverty in the process.

For the ancient Egyptians, who viewed their history in terms of monuments and monument making, the almost mythical reign of Djoser was regarded as a time of great wisdom and achievement. The sole architect of these buildings, they believed, was Imhotep, known in Djoser's time as sculptor-builder and chief minister of the land. He was later revered as a god of medicine and wisdom, a deity to whom the scribes would sprinkle a few drops of water from their ink palettes before they started to write.

The Step Pyramid with its west face in shadow

The Step Pyramid enclosure has only one entrance, a slot-shaped door-way at one end of the long wall that overlooks Memphis. Above this entrance is a watchman's walkway, and behind the door beneath is a long colonnade, now restored to its original appearance, in semi-darkness. The contrast is extraordinary: from the bright desert and white exterior walls of the compound to the shaded hall of stone columns, each one of which is carefully sculpted as a bundle of reeds; models, it may be imagined, of similar columns that once supported the palaces and store rooms of Memphis.

Every culture fashions its images of death from the landscape that it inhabits and in this respect the ancient Egyptians were no exception. Death was often described by them as a continuous journey, a voyage, therefore, on a great river like that of the pilgrimage of the dead to Abydos. Thus the fields of reeds that lined the river's banks became an aphorism for dying – the medium between life and death. In life these fields of reeds were one of the great game reserves of the country and the court nobles speared fish and hunted ducks, even, on occasion harpooned hippopotami in them. In the world of death these same animals became associated with the forces of the underworld that had to be fought and overcome in an endless series of magical contests. As we 'pass over' or 'pass away' so the Egyptians passed through these fields of reeds on their way to burial and it was most fitting, therefore, that Djoser's architects made a hall of reeds for the dead king to pass through on the way to his burial under the pyramid. The entrance to the royal mortuary enclosure became, quite literally, the medium between life and death, this world and the next.

Walk around Djoser's buildings and you will soon realize that this archi-tecture was not meant for the living. The paths and doorways that connect the many different areas are small; certainly they were not designed as processional ways or as the locations for large assemblies of people. Furthermore, these beautiful buildings are all solid, their doors and the simple wicket-fence barriers are immovable stone imitations of the kinds used in shelters made of reed, palms and mud brick that, surely, were inhabited by the living. Yet these buildings are not mere models of their organic prototypes, stone simply taking the place of wood, but are made of small rectangular blocks that one or two men might lift. These blocks were built up in regular abstract rows to form the outline of the architecture which was then carved to imitate the surface forms of 'real' buildings.

Djoser's architects had elegantly petrified the forms of the buildings that housed the government of Egypt and like models of the buildings of Whitehall and Westminster they symbolized the structure of the nation. Unlike their Western counterparts however, they were holy, shrine-like

The entrance colonnade of the Step Pyramid enclosure

buildings that held their political significance as a religious reality. This most beautiful architecture, neither propagandistic nor processional was not for this world but for the next. It is architecture made for the spirit of the dead king so that he might continue the ritual activities of this world in his afterlife; so that, for all eternity, the royal spirit would spread its unifying and fertilizing power throughout the land.

From just a few signs something of the purposes of this lifesized model of the state of Egypt may be gleaned – mostly elegant decorations that hint at similar themes common in the later architecture of ancient Egypt. Lines of sight, for instance, were of great significance in Djoser's enclosure. On a wall directly facing the entrance doorway, though nearly 150 feet behind it, was set a high frieze of stone cobras their heads reared and ready to strike. Later, these snakes became the symbol of royal power and protection that, when set onto the forehead of representations of the king, identified him as the ruler of Egypt. Other sightlines through the buildings display sculptures of the plants that symbolized the traditional dual division of Egypt into the Upper and Lower Kingdoms. The forms of these heraldic plants were used as columns by Djoser's architects, and they are the first decorated columns in the world. The superb workmanship almost hides the fact that the columns, perhaps through the architects' lack of confidence, are not free standing but are still engaged to the wall that stands with them. They decorate two separate courtyards, each containing one tall building made in the form of a large open hall.

As you would expect of a monument that underwent so many architectural transformations before arriving at its final form, Djoser's pyramid is a mass of structural changes, though all are neatly contained inside the bland exterior of the final version. Underneath the mass of the pyramid is a maze of tunnels and chambers that contain the burial arrangement of at least twelve people including, perhaps, Djoser's predecessor who, it has been suggested, may have initiated the original structure under the pyramid. These subterranean tunnels – streets of burial apartments – were filled with the impedimenta of the royal dead. Stacked in many of the corridors, looking like the crushed shells of dinosaur eggs, were hundreds of thousands of stone vases. Many were already centuries old when they were placed under Djoser's pyramid; they are momentoes of earlier kings. Mostly, they are very finely made, some engraved with inscriptions that may hold the keys to the solutions of some of the many problems that these early periods of ancient history have left for us in such abundance.

Stone-vase manufacture in Egypt diminished considerably at the same time as the introduction of the potter's wheel. This simple machine enabled large vessels to be made quickly and easily in clay, and dealt the

Previous pages Part of a court in the Step Pyramid complex that contains two rows of dummy buildings; an elaborate architectural environment designed about 2655 B.C.

death blow to the fine ceramic and vase industries of the previous millenia. Henceforth, the pottery of Egypt, though always pleasing, was basically utilitarian. However, the reservoir of skill and sensitivity gained in working hard stone bore dramatic fruit with the birth of stone architecture. Already this sculptural sensitivity to stone appears in its finest and purest form in Djoser's great mortuary complex. The later architecture of the Old Kingdom greatly expanded the range of stone types used until the buildings appear like great necklaces that span the bases of the royal pyramids.

At his death King Djoser was placed in a large granite chamber under the centre of his pyramid, a strange sarcophagus room sealed ingeniously with a round plug of granite shaped like a gigantic cork. Two Englishmen, excavating during the 1920s for the Egyptian government, found a mummified foot in this chamber which, they believed, was that of Djoser himself. It was a rare trophy and an interesting example of embalming from such an early period.

Djoser had another large tomb built for himself in his enclosure sited behind the great frieze of snakes that were attached to the southern wall. Battered on its sides like the pyramid and with a gently curving roof, which may also have echoed the royal tombs of the Umm el Ga'ab, this tomb was a rectangle, some 250 feet long and 40 feet wide. At its centre the excavators discovered a sand-filled pit, a great rectangular hole which, as they discovered when they proceeded to excavate it, was nearly 90 feet deep! At its bottom was a smaller version of the granite tomb room that lay under the pyramid. The proportions and the disposition of this second monument had affinities with an earlier mud-brick tomb built for Djoser in a cemetery near This in Upper Egypt.

Access could also be had to this so-called Southern Tomb by a long sloping stairway that passed over the burial chamber at the bottom of the pit. Beyond this lay another small maze of corridors and passages, some of which contained a series of decorated niches. These too were made in imitation of bundled reeds and other similar plant forms but here the patterns were inlaid with fine, small, bright blue-glazed tiles. These are among the oldest and finest extant examples and under the name of 'Egyptian faience' have become a trademark of the ancient culture.

In the three niches that were set into these deep and glittering galleries were limestone reliefs showing the king engaged in the ceremony of the royal jubilee. This was a series of rites designed to revive magically the royal potency after a lengthy period of rule. Interestingly, there are some striking parallels among many tribal peoples of Africa today. Many of the buildings of Djoser's compound seem to have been made for the same rites. Thus the spirit of the dead king could perform these rituals for all eternity, rituals that were first pictured by the ancient Egyptians on some of the small ivory fragments that Petrie recovered from the royal tombs of the Umm el Ga'ab.

A similar group of chambers was built under Djoser's pyramid and it is interesting that the depth of the shafts of the Southern Tomb and the burial chamber under the pyramid are equal. On a modern plan they form an obvious architectural entity although the precise ritual function that these two graves served still awaits explanation. Perhaps we shall have the answer after the excavation of similar compounds that lie out in the desert beyond the Step Pyramid, which have not yet been touched by archeologists. Indeed, one third of Djoser's enclosure is still buried in drifted sand and that too might hold some surprises.

The two underground galleries with their blue panelled reliefs are among the finest surviving sights of ancient Egypt, yet they have always been difficult of access and stand in total darkness. It is truly an extraordinary experience to visit these cool blue tiled chambers that lie deep under the desert sand. Obviously they were not designed for display – and this is typical of many of the finest products of the ancient nation. Many of the sculptures brought from Egypt and now lavishly exhibited in museums were taken from windowless stone boxes where, it was assumed, the statues would stand for all eternity. Yet they were made with extraordinary care and attention. This aesthetic conception of a plain exterior enclosing a complex and powerful hidden centre – rather like a modern power station or nuclear reactor – was a very common one in Egyptian architecture. The large temples, for example, were also screened from the outside world by massive, high enclosing walls that hid all evidence of the ritual activities that were constantly taking place inside. At the Step Pyramid this concept was epitomized by a small neatly made stone building shaped like a pillbox that had been built into the bottom of the north side of the pyramid.

Inside this box, archeologists discovered a magnificent statue of the king, seated and facing south up the Nile Valley. This *serdab* – as all such statue rooms are called – had originally been completely enclosed, and Djoser's statue, the first great masterpiece of ancient Egyptian sculpture, was visible only through two small holes drilled through the stone block that confronted the statue's face as it stared into the darkness. Through the two small holes the royal mortuary priests would blow smoke of smouldering incense towards the face of the king. In common with most of the world's religions the ancient Egyptians believed that incense was a valuable medium between men and the gods.

With these splendid buildings and sculptures of Djoser's reign it is apparent that the ancient Egyptian culture was established as a style that would endure in the land. The reliefs that show the king performing the ritual acts of the jubilee, the fragments of finely cut inscriptions, and the sculpture that has survived, all show the measured care and authority that is typical of the later mature style. But in common with most examples of the arts of formative eras these pieces are all charged with an especial fire, a tremendous vigour and freshness.

For many years modern scholarship has been occupied in attempting to discover which of the several tombs of the Archaic kings actually held the physical remains of the monarch, and this is a complex question, for even in later periods many kings built 'cenotaphs' while they themselves were undoubtedly buried elsewhere. Many courtiers, too, followed this royal precedent and had elaborate tomb chambers and chapels built, although they were actually buried in small shafts close to the royal tomb. Some inscriptions tell us that the spirits of these people would look out from their empty tomb chapels across the river to the cities of the living, and that they could also smell the perfume of the sweet scented crops by the Nile brought to them on the evening breezes. These dummy tombs enabled the spirits of the dead to be close to places that held especial significance for them. From their tombs, spread about the Nile Valley, the kings could spread their power in the land and observe its progress throughout the year. As peripatetic as the king had been in life, so would his spirit be in death, journeying from tomb to tomb, travelling with the sun across the sky and visiting the regions of the underworld as the sun passed through to reappear on the eastern horizon.

Djoser brought the royal presence of death to one place. And by bringing together the royal tombs and cenotaphs on the Sakkara plateau he literally gathered the nation about him in death. It was the beginning of a massive focusing of royal power in one location that reached an extraordinary climax during the next dynasty. The likes of most of Djoser's buildings, however, innovative in size, material and ritual purpose as they were, were never made again. They remain, therefore, unique; some of the gentlest and most exquisite architecture ever made: the deified Imhotep has made one of the magical places of mankind.

CHAPTER SIX
PYRAMID

From the reign of Djoser until the beginning of the New Kingdom almost every king of substance and authority was buried under a pyramid. At the end of this long tradition the splendid visions of the earlier dynasties had shrunk to monuments of poorly built steep-sided mud brick that were often no larger than about 40 feet square, but a thousand years before, pyramids had been measured in hundreds of feet, their masonry in millions of tons. The largest of all, the Great Pyramid on the Plateau of Giza, near modern Cairo, is still the biggest stone building ever made by man and one of the most accurately constructed. It was built less than one hundred years after Djoser's craftsmen had started their work on the Step Pyramid.

Singularly, the kings of the Third Dynasty who followed Djoser to the throne have not left any finished monuments – though there might still be some surprises lying under the desert sands at Sakkara. It was at the beginning of the Fourth Dynasty, in the desert north of the older monuments, that pyramid building on a quite unprecedented scale was started. These Fourth Dynasty monuments are the finest of the pyramids: seldom do they measure less than 350 feet along their sides and most are double that. After this time there was an immediate reduction in size and quality of construction that continued throughout the rest of the Old Kingdom. During the Middle Kingdom, however, the pyramids once again reached the colossal measurements of their forerunners, but these monuments were of carefully buttressed mud-brick cased with stone, some of which had been quarried from the monuments of their predecessors to fit over the fresh mud brick like the shells of hermit crabs. Later, this fine stone skin was removed by other parasitical masons and the soft mud-brick cores have now eroded into unrecognizable shapes that require the paper plans of archeologists to recover something of their former magnificence in the mind's eye.

Despite this decay, there is little doubt about what the Middle Kingdom rulers thought of their monuments: 'the High and Beautiful', 'the Mighty',

The pyramids of Giza at a distance of some nine miles

The Giza pyramid field. The Great Pyramid, built by King Cheops, is the largest of the three

'the Pure', 'the Peaceful' are some of the names of these sad ruins. Several of these epithets recall the days of the Fourth Dynasty: 'Rising in Splendour' for example, is a title similar to that held by two of the largest monuments of that time. The scanty inscriptions connected with the Old Kingdom monuments also show, perhaps, a feeling of exultation at the power in the state, and some of the names of the Fourth Dynasty stone-hauling gangs reflect this same feeling; 'Sceptre Gang' (a reference to an emblem of kingship), 'Vigorous Gang' and, appropriately enough, inscribed on a block of the Great Pyramid, 'Craftsmen Gang', after which is added, perhaps in wonder at the monument that they were making, 'How powerful is the White Crown of Cheops!' (i.e. the organization of the state.)

Cheops, or Khufu to give him his Egyptian name, was the king for whom the Great Pyramid was made. He was the second king of the Fourth Dynasty and reigned from about 2589 B.C. for a period of twenty-three years. The construction of his pyramid must have taken up most of those years. What extraordinary confidence possessed the architects of this great pyramid as they strode over the bare desert plateau marking out the size of the projected monument! At that time they were committing the primary resources of their nation for generations. That such extraordinary optimism was sometimes misplaced is seen at less-visited sites where the construction of similarly vast monuments hardly progressed beyond the

76

cutting of a huge trench that was to hold the royal burial chamber. This stopping of the work, it is assumed, was due to the premature death of the king.

But such cancellations were not the rule. In the reign of Cheop's father, Sneferu, no less than three mighty pyramids were built south of Sakkara, each one of which, in its size, comes close to rivalling the single monument of his son. It is interesting to observe that the buildings that accompanied these three pyramids were extremely simple, that all the architectural ritual of Djoser's great complex was discarded, freeing the workforce and its resources, allowing it to concentrate on the pyramid itself. It was during the reign of Sneferu that the final form of the pyramid, the straight-sided version that covered over the stepped structures of Djoser's monument, was established and this survived right through the monuments of the Old and Middle Kingdoms, built in a seventy-mile band down the western bank of the Nile near Memphis. Moreover, it was during Sneferu's reign that the considerable technical problems involved in building such enormous structures were overcome while at this same time, the nation was welded into a veritable race of tomb builders. It was a potent legacy that was eagerly grasped by Sneferu's son.

For, despite the three majestic monuments of Sneferu – the combined

The pyramids at Dashur built by King Sneferu, father of Cheops

masonry of which has been estimated at some nine million tons – the pyramid field *par excellence* must surely be the Plateau of Giza. There, during the greater part of the Fourth Dynasty, multitudes of masons' gangs chipped and chiselled at the landscape to re-form it into the pyramids of three kings, and into hundreds of other, smaller monuments. It was a grand gesture that, stretching out over the landscape, printed the hand of man next to the forms of God. These mountainous efforts must have taken virtually the entire energy of the nation which, according to modern estimates, stood at that time at about 1.6 million people. The pyramids, therefore, *are* the history of the Fourth Dynasty. But for historians who like to chew over family relationships, battles, treaties and all the normal burdens of history, the period remains practically an empty book. Yet these people left buildings as finely made as watches and so large that they defy imagination.

Indeed, the accuracy of Cheop's pyramid is no less phenomenal than its bulk. The maximum error in the four sides at their bases, the mean length of which is about 755.8 feet, is just 8 inches. The faces of the pyramid, sited on the points of the compass to provide a fixed point with which to check the progress of the work, show a maximum error at the base of a little over one twelfth of a degree. The right-angles at the corners are equally precise: the largest single error in them amounting to less than one twentieth of a degree. As are all the others, the Great Pyramid is virtually a solid structure composed, in the most part of blocks of limestone numbering, it has been estimated, some 2,300,000 averaging $2\frac{1}{2}$ tons each. It has also been calculated that with eight-man gangs each moving one of these blocks from the quarries to the pyramid that the entire structure could have been assembled by 100,000 men in 'less than twenty years'.

In some ways, this extraordinarily intense activity, which continued on the Giza Plateau for the better part of a century, can be likened to the cathedral building of medieval Europe – an expression of faith that is reflected in the quality of the architecture, the activity of building as an act of worship. In this sense, the pyramids may be seen as the memorials of a vital process, and it was this *process* that was the real core of the enter- prise. We are merely left with the results. But there is one vital difference. The accuracy of the pyramids was not prompted by sentiments of piety but was the result of necessarily strict controls instituted so that the form of the monument would retain its accuracy during the lengthy period of its construction. Such plain geometric shapes as the pyramids will clearly show any deviations from true, and their extraordinary accuracy is an incredible demonstration of the strength of the ancient state.

This building programme, then, was a demonstration of the successful application of the mechanisms of state. And, as the accuracy of the

The Great Pyramid of Giza at sunset

pyramids was maintained during the long periods of construction, so the culture of Egypt was itself maintained throughout thousands of years by the similarly strict application of rules and methods. As they built their pyramids so the Egyptians built their state. It was a dramatic climax to the culture that was made during the first two dynasties and it left Egypt with a cultural self-confidence and self-awareness that survived the tribulations of more than 2,000 years of history.

There is, now, broad agreement among scholars concerning the outline of the techniques that were used to build the pyramids, though many details, especially of the methods used for the initial survey and the subsequent geometric controls, remain obscure. One old theory that has collapsed following fresh research into the ancient flood levels in the Nile Valley was the proposition that stone used in the pyramids was brought to Giza on barges that were able to cross the Nile Valley at the time of the annual inundation. It now appears that the shallow depth of the annual floods during the Old Kingdom would not have allowed the passage of barges of sufficient draught to carry such huge blocks. It is more likely, therefore, that special canals were dug from the Nile bank to the bottom of the desert ridge and the stone barges came up these specially constructed waterways to the foot of the pyramid.

Of course, the Nile was an essential transportation system for the enormous tonnages of hard stone that were brought to the pyramids from the deserts and the cataracts of Upper Egypt. Aswan granite was especially favoured as a finishing stone, often used to line the interior chambers and corridors of the pyramids and also for the massive lintels that spread the huge loads of the masonry above the burial chambers. The fine white limestone used for the outer surfaces of many of the pyramids was brought from the quarries of Tura on the eastern bank of the river opposite Giza. The bulk of the limestone used in the pyramids however, was quarried from the surrounding plateaux.

The huge stone blocks were handled by gangs using sledges, rollers, ropes and rocking platforms that, with the use of wedges, could be used to raise the blocks small distances. For the final ascent to their position in the pyramid the blocks were dragged by the gangs up ramps of mud brick which, when they were lubricated with water, would have had a surface almost as slippery as ice. Traces of such ramps are still in position by their pyramids, and other more complete examples have been cleared from later temples where they were used in the same way. A New Kingdom papyrus preserves the mathematical formula used for a rough calculation of the volumes of such enormous constructions.

Building the ramps to allow the transportation of large blocks of stone as much as 600 feet up to the top of a pyramid, would have been equal to the effort of constructing the pyramid itself, and this fact has sometimes been used as an argument against their use at the larger monuments: that no builder would ever employ such an uneconomic method. But it is false to judge these ancient buildings by the rules of modern economics. There are very many instances where the ancient Egyptians devoted long periods of time and much skill to tasks which by modern standards would not be acceptable. And this is a basic reason why many of the products of the ancient Egyptians are so profoundly different from those of modern cultures. The Egyptians made their monuments for reasons other than those that govern the work of most modern architects and artists: as the economist John Maynard Keynes succinctly observed, 'Two pyramids, two masses for the dead are twice as good as one; not so two railways from London to York'.

Two cultures, ancient and modern, have expended quite different amounts of time and effort on quite different aspects of their architectures, and they have, therefore, developed two quite separate technologies. In the process, the Western world has largely lost the skills of managing large numbers of manual workers which the ancient Egyptians possessed to a remarkable degree. Further, modern notions of what is practical are severely limited by factors of time. Our methods of moving blocks as large as those used at Giza, for example, require engineering skills that, ideally, will resolve the problem at a touch of a button. Yet in Egypt today, the villagers employed for manual labour on archeological excavations still easily shift ancient blocks about with great skill. They have a sensitivity towards the special properties of friction and balance that such loads have, they share a confidence in each other, and work easily in group rhythms. How much more skilful must the ancient gangs of Giza have been, with a hundred years of experience behind them!

After the Fourth Dynasty the royal pyramids were greatly reduced in size, and paradoxically it is this dynasty, an age virtually devoid of recorded political history, an age of national absorption in building and architecture, that is often regarded as the apex of the ancient Egyptian culture. However, with the reduction in size, the accompanying facilities became greatly elaborated. Texts were inscribed in the chambers inside the pyramids, and the temples that had always accompanied the monuments became increasingly complex and lavishly decorated: theological exposition partly replaced the sheer bulk of the Fourth Dynasty monuments.

The natural conclusion of this tendency was reached during the Twelfth Dynasty. One of the pyramid temples of that era has since entered legend, as the Labyrinth, one of the seven wonders of the world which, as an architectural vision, slipped across the sea to Crete to become the hunting ground of Jason and the Minos bull. In their architectural convolutions, especially the complex security systems that surrounded the pyramids' burial chambers, these Middle Kingdom monuments seem more worldly wise than the Old Kingdom models on which they were based. Some of them contained hydraulic mechanisms that worked with sand, blind

The pyramid of Amenemhet III of the Middle Kingdom, and the ruin
of its mortuary temple that is sometimes identified as the Labyrinth

passages leading prospecting robbers away from the burial chamber – in fact, much of the paraphenalia so beloved of Hollywood epics.

The Middle Kingdom kings were well aware that the massive yet simple security devices of the Old Kingdom pyramids had, without exception, failed their owners during the anarchic time of the First Intermediate Period; the kings who had supervised the building of the Giza pyramids were now 'cast out upon the high ground', as an ancient scribe wrote of their dismal fate. The elaborate security systems of the Middle Kingdom pyramids are an architectural expression of the physical insecurity of the kings themselves; anarchy, after all, had proved that the god-king was not

The ruined pyramid of the Fifth Dynasty king, Sahure, at Abusir

invulnerable. However, these extraordinarily ingenious systems, too, failed their hopeful owners, for with the exception of some pyramids whose burial chambers have been submerged with the rising of the Nile's water table, all were robbed in distant antiquity.

One of the longest tales that has survived from ancient Egypt describes the death of one Middle Kingdom monarch, Senusert I:

> Year 30, third month of the inundation, day 7: the god ascended to his horizon. The king of Upper and Lower Egypt flew to heaven and united with the sun-disk, the divine body merging with its maker. Then the residence [of the king] was hushed; hearts grieved; the great portals were shut; the courtiers were head-on-knee; the people moaned.

If the construction of the pyramids had special significance for the Egyptian people, then the death of the kings whose tombs had been prepared inside them was a national crisis to be overcome only with the aid of ancient rite and ritual. Many of the architectural forms which had previously contained these rituals had been discarded by the Fourth Dynasty pyramid builders, who concentrated their efforts on perfecting the form of the royal grave. However, the substance of the earlier burial rites and beliefs were contained in a series of texts preserved in papyrus rolls and when the size of the pyramid decreased during the Fifth Dynasty, these texts were carved on the walls of the burial chambers and of the rooms that preceded them inside the pyramids. The complex symbolism of the texts provides a magnificent foil to the relatively new simplicities of the royal architecture.

> Sky rains, stars darken
> The vaults quiver, earth's bones tremble,
> The [planets] stand still
> At seeing [king] Unas rise as power,
> A god who lives on his fathers,
> Who feeds on his mothers!

After the cosmic drama of the royal death, the king rises to heaven to eat the gods, his fathers and his mothers! This image of a cannibal king eating the gods to ingest their qualities is not present in dynastic religion and reflects much older beliefs. The resurrection of another king is described in a text as though his burial had been a dismembered interment placed directly into the earth:

> Oho! Oho! Rise up, O [king] Teti!
> Take your head,
> Collect your bones,
> Gather your limbs,
> Shake the earth from your flesh!

In fact, the king's body would have been swathed in mummy bandages and placed in a fine sarcophagus at the centre of his pyramid.

The oldest versions of much of this fascinating collection of spells, prayers and rubrics that are presently known are carved in the chambers of a small pyramid at Sakkara built close to the walls of the Step Pyramid complex. This 'edition' has since been augmented by many others found in pyramids and in the tomb chapels of private citizens. As in their creation stories, the ancient Egyptians use multitudes of interlocking images in these texts to establish one single fact: that the dead king was now one with his family, the Gods; and through the survival of the king after death the continuance of Egypt was ensured. In modern translation the texts are often very beautiful and frequently the most incomprehensible or elusive passages in terms of rational explanation are more truly suggestive of the central mysteries of the ancient faith than those which are prosaically understandable. All the texts were composed in a language filled with the imagery of the Nile Valley and draw on its landscapes, and its flora and fauna. They also tell of customs, which for the ancient Egyptians were a central part of their ancient faith, but for us are represented only by elegant archaic artefacts. With complex constructions, rich in metaphor and allusion, the texts touch the mystery of the royal resurrection. In a typically oblique explanation of the form of his *Cantos*, Ezra Pound has some lines which, although from a different age, seem to grasp at similar notions!

> . . . say I take your whole bag of tricks,
> Let in your quirks and tweeks, and say the thing's an art-form,
> Your Sordello, and that the modern world
> Needs such a rag-bag to stuff all its thought in;
> Say that I dump my catch, shiny and silvery
> As fresh sardines slapping and slipping on the marginal cobbles?
> (I stand before the booth, the speech; but the truth
> Is inside this discourse – this book is full of the marrow of wisdom.)

The ancient 'book' too – called the Pyramid Texts – attempts to grasp this marrow of wisdom and to use it to the advantage of the dead king. A dominant theme was the royal death seen as a journey to heaven, a journey the king undertook by any vehicle that the ancient scribes might devise. So the king might go to heaven as incense smoke, as a cloud of dust, flying like a bird, walking up a ladder, or jumping like a grasshopper; and in these many guises, he would meet the gods. One king, Unas, travelled as a conqueror, he 'seizes the sky and cleaves its fabric'; other images have him tripping lightly into the presence of the gods as a dancing pigmy. Another describes him as a scribe of Dickensian obsequiousness!

> Unas is Gods' steward behind the mansion of Re [house of the gods]
> Born of wish-of-the-Gods,
> Unas squats before him,
> Unas opens his boxes,
> Unas unseals his decrees
> Unas seals his dispatches,
> Unas sends his messengers who tire not,
> Unas does what Unas is told.

Anything, it seems, is good enough to get to heaven.

Very little is known of the detail of the royal funeral, of its rites, rituals and ceremonies, although several attempts have been made to reconstruct them from the Pyramid Texts. Despite the fact that some of the more prosaic of these literary disinterments have been described by one authority as 'being similar to making a card index of the words of the High Mass and attempting to write a history of the Jews from the results', some of the buildings in which the rituals were performed have survived and, despite their sim-

Overleaf *A restored section of the causeway of Unas that ran from a lower temple up to the temple at the foot of the royal pyramid. Built at Sakkara in the Fifth Dynasty*

plicity, the almost modern marriage of form to function can tell us a great deal of their purpose.

The king was first brought to a temple built by the edge of the cultivation at the bottom of the desert scarp. The royal corpse was probably transported along the same canals that had been used to bring the stone up to the plateau of his pyramid. The temple, doubtless surrounded by a riverside field of reeds, was usually complex in shape and its numerous halls and chambers suggest a variety of ritual functions.

From the Nile-side temples where, it has been suggested the kings may have been mummified and encoffined, the royal body was placed on a funerary sledge which was dragged up a long, covered stone causeway towards the pyramid. These enormous, well built structures have since, almost without exception, been largely ruined. The walls of the causeways were decorated with finely made reliefs whose subject matter ranged as widely as those carved at later dates in the royal temples. The causeway of Unas, for example, was over a mile long and was completely cased in heavy stone – a long dark corridor running through the desert. The only light in the passage came from a single slit that ran continuously along the centre of the roof and which must have lit the procession like a single dazzling striplight. The ancient architects expended much time and resources ensuring that the royal progress should *not* be observed. And this is not surprising when it is understood that most religious processions, slow and irregularly moving rituals, were usually performed for the benefit of society as a whole, and that the special role of *observer* is essentially a modern one, born of organized processions of military display.

From the semi-gloom of the causeway the royal coffins and the accompanying party emerged into the dazzling brightness of a temple court at the foot of the pyramid. Since ancient times most of the external layer of the pyramids has been stripped off, but originally they were smooth white objects that must have appeared quite alien as they stood in the sand, gleaming in the Nile Valley sunlight. This second temple also had extensive ritual facilities and was generally built of the finest of hard stones – the one at the Great Pyramid, for example, has a huge pavement of black basalt, an incredibly dense material. From this temple, used for the rituals of the cult of the dead king, sometimes for many hundreds of years after his death, the royal mummy was taken to the entrance of his pyramid. From there the burial party, by now bent over in the small narrow passageways, moved down towards the royal burial chamber.

This, the activation of the pyramid, was for those ancient people as powerful an act as the insertion of rods into an atomic reactor. So intense was the identification of the dead with their pyramids that, in some instances, the name of the pyramid also became the name of the dead person. For us of course, this is equally true; Cheops has become his pyramid: no pyramid, no Cheops.

It seems extraordinary that after all the immense labour and organization required to build the pyramids that the Egyptians eventually sent the king to his grave along tunnels that are often too small to stand in. In no manner could a procession have passed with any dignity through a pyramid: the interment was, in fact, a task that must have been primarily performed by the gang of workmen who sealed the passages and closed the lid of the royal sarcophagus. So small were the spaces left for these operations that there would have been little room for ritual. Like the building of the pyramid, this work too *was* the ritual, the labour *was* the rite.

The Pyramid Texts that decorate many of these subterranean apartments appear to have an order in their positioning on the walls. They describe something of the belief that surround the last acts of burial. In the texts engraved at the end of the descending corridors that lead to the hearts of the pyramids are descriptions of the king taking on the identity of animals that, for the Egyptians, had the special attributes of virility and power – essential requirements for the processes of royal self-regeneration. He is identified both as a bull and as a crocodile emerging from the flood. To enter the anteroom to the burial chamber the party first shot the bolts of the door, which were identified in the texts as the penis of a baboon – the animal that in its natural habitat is the first to greet the rising sun with an animated display of jumping and arm waving. The doorbolts were signs of great virility and potential power; clearly we are coming close to the heart of the tomb.

Passing through this low entrance the burial party could now stand in the high-vaulted anteroom. This was often covered in texts, all carefully cut in vertical columns of hieroglyphs that were painted blue straight onto the white limestone walls. They tell of the king's journey to the company of the gods: he comes like lightning; he flies as a goose; a ferryman takes him across to the land of the gods; the metaphors roll on and on. There are also descriptions of the king meeting the gods, of the royal reception in heaven. On the low doorway between the anteroom and the burial chamber the texts seem to relate to a more specific, earthbound ritual. This is the Ceremony of the Red Jars, by which the enemies of the king were destroyed in the breaking of pottery. This most ancient rite, paralleled by customs in many religions that also centre upon the destruction of some possession at the interment, still figured in the burial of Tutankhamen in his tomb in the Valley of the Kings more than 1,000 years after the last burial in a royal pyramid. Other rituals, involving the breaking of pottery inscribed with hated names, and sometimes curses, were employed by the ancient Egyptians as a magical way of destroying real enemies.

The texts on this low doorway also describe the king finally being welcomed to his sarcophagus by the goddess Nut. She is his mother, the night sky, and on later royal sarcophagi and sometimes on the wooden coffins which fitted inside them, she is drawn on the lids as a young woman dressed in a long robe spangled with the night stars. Having, on his death, taken the identity of his father, the young king will lay with the goddess to engender himself: the royal resurrection. In one of these texts the king tells the goddess that he has left earthly matters behind him:

> This Unas comes to you, O Nut,
> This Unas comes to you, O Nut,
> He has consigned his father to the earth,
> He has left Horus behind him.
> Grown are his falcon wings,
> Plumes of the holy hawk;
> His power has brought him,
> His magic has equipped him!

and the goddess replies:

> Make your seat in heaven,
> Among the stars of heaven,
> For you are the Evening Star
> You shall look down on Osiris,
> As he commands the spirits,
> While you stand far from him;
> You are not among them,
> you shall not be among them!

The royal sarcophagi stand at the rear walls of their burial chambers and were as carefully made as the pyramids themselves. They are marvels of stone cutting, precise to within hundredths of an inch, accurately angled, their surfaces cut as flat as sheets of glass. So accurate are they, indeed, that in modern times the sarcophagus of the Great Pyramid has spawned a whole fake mythology that portrays it as the key to a sad collection of 'ancient mysteries' whereby the pyramids are transformed into machines for fortune telling or performing trivial pseudo-scientific tricks.

For the ancient Egyptians, however, the sarcophagus was, quite literally, a house for the dead. Several of them were shaped like archaic tombs and palaces, models in granite of the power of the king. The royal mummies were placed inside their sarcophagi already encased in coffins and wrapped tightly in bandages before they were brought into their pyramids. It is likely that in the internal chambers of the pyramids were placed some of the personal possessions of the king, as well as statues of him and of the gods – so that the dead monarch was literally in their presence. It is very unlikely, however, that the pyramids ever held a wealth of golden treasure like that found in Tutankhamen's tomb.

The texts that decorate the walls of the pyramids' burial chambers mainly continue the descriptions of the kings' introduction to heaven and the gods; others, in the outer chambers, give simple spells against snakes, demons and other hazards of the afterlife. Particular to the burial chambers, however, are the traditional lists of offerings of food, clothing, weapons, and other equipment, all written into elegant long columns, so that the king, in death, would never want for the basic necessities. In several of the pyramids these texts give way, in the area around the sarcophagus, to elaborate wall decorations which represent the doorways on the façades of the archaic palaces and tombs. These highly decorative panels were the medium through which the royal spirit would pass to reach the land of the living once again – its doorways to the world. There were similar panels at the focus of the royal mortuary temples where, presumably, they supplied the spirits of the kings with access to their cult and the offerings that had been made to them. Later, this same device, though somewhat simplified, appeared on the royal sarcophagi in the Valley of the Kings and these 'false doors' as they are called are also found wherever a 'looking glass' was required for contact between this world and the next.

The 'false door' in the burial chamber of the pyramid of King Unas, decorated with the typical patterns of the 'palace façade'. The two lines of vertical text to its left are a small section of the Pyramid Texts

CHAPTER SEVEN

BUREAUCRATICS

At sunrise, the Great Pyramid of Giza casts its huge triangular shadow over the western cemetery of the royal courtiers, their tombs lying on the desert plateau like the regular pattern of a chocolate bar. Each of the hundred or so tombs is much the same: a few are unusually large, a few are very small, but most of them are regular, battered rectangular prisms of stone around 23.5 m long, 9.5 m wide and about 4 m high. Similar tombs of various sizes are arranged along the other sides of the pyramid, and smaller and less carefully organized cemeteries are attached to the other two royal pyramids on the plateau. These rows of tombs show evidence of the same precise organization, the same degree of order, that is apparent in the pyramids themselves.

All the tombs of Cheop's courtiers are made of blocks of the same stone as the Great Pyramid above them and, in their way, are as simple and as excellent in their design, each one accurately placed in the grid of streets and alleyways. By a corner of each tomb there is a false door and, sometimes, a niche that once held a slab of fine white Tura limestone which bore a relief showing the dead person receiving offerings at the tomb. Some of the tombs have small stone chapels attached to them, which hold reliefs and sculptures of the tomb owner and members of his family. A large number of the tombs are now anonymous having lost all trace of decoration or inscription.

In the top of each tomb there is a deep square shaft and the burial chamber runs from its bottom. Each burial contained a large rectangular sarcophagus and sometimes a meal, laid on plates, was left on the floor in front of it. Jars of pottery found in these chambers probably once held food and drink. In the thickness of the mud-brick wall that closed off the burial chamber from the entrance shaft, which at the time of burial was filled with sand and stones, were placed sculptured heads of limestone – portraits, perhaps, of the tomb's owner.

As the court served the king in life, so it continued its function after

Nobles' tombs in the western cemetery at the foot of the Great Pyramid

death. And this cemetery held not only the royal courtiers and members of the royal family but also the governors of the provinces of Egypt. The tombs, though massive and precise, held little of the wealth that, presumably, surrounded their owners in life. The limestone portrait heads, however, are marvels of sensitivity – perhaps some of the finest sculptures ever made by the ancient Egyptians. Most of them have had their ears smashed in some as yet unknown ritual. Many of the reliefs in the tombs are equal in quality to the limestone portraits; what there is for us to see in this world of giants is elegant, discriminating, and truly noble. Although this semi-anonymous court may hardly emerge as individuals from the gloom of the tomb-streets in the shadow of the Great Pyramid, the traces that are left tell of a thoughtful, sensitive people, who appreciated fine craftsmanship.

The few texts of the period that have survived are involved with these tombs, with eternity and with the offices of the dead. One describes the legal details of the establishment of a mortuary foundation, supported by grants of land and town given by the king, to endow the cult of the dead. The details, such as provisions for the death or retirement of the managing priests and the penalties for violations of the agreement, are precise. There are few biographical particulars in these tomb texts beyond titles and a description of the family relationship to the king. It is a feudalism, with

all its responsibilities and interdependencies, honed to the very bone, a stripping down to the barest forms, that is typical of so much of ancient Egyptian thought, but always expressed in the language of solid objects – here architecture and sculpture – and never in the abstract.

All the resources of the royal monopolies might be put at the disposal of a courtier whom the king wanted buried in the cemetery of his nobles; a unique text from the tomb of Debhen tells exactly of the circumstances and organization of such a gift. Debhen was the governor of an important Upper Egyptian town and a court functionary in the reign of Mycerinos, who built the smallest of the three royal pyramids at Giza. In this text, which is in the chapel of his tomb, Debhen tells us of the history of his 'house of eternity'.

> As for this tomb, it was the King of Upper and Lower Egypt, Menkaure [Mycerinos] who caused that it be made when his majesty was upon the road beside the Queen's pyramid [one of the small pyramids built beside the royal monuments at Giza] in order to inspect the work upon his pyramid 'Divine is Menkaure'. There came the naval commander [of the stone barges?] and the two High Priests of Memphis [planners?] and the workmen standing upon the pyramid to inspect the work.
>
> And his Majesty commanded to clear a place of rubbish for this tomb [Debhen's tomb is in quarries close by the pyramid and there must have been

Left *The Giza pyramid field at sunrise*

Right *Limestone head of a princess from her tomb by the Great Pyramid (Kunsthistoriches Museum, Vienna)*

large quantities of stone chippings lying around, as there still are]. His Majesty commanded that the two treasurers of the god should come; that there should be brought stone from Tura to clothe the [royal pyramid] temples together with two false doors and a front for [Debhen's] tomb: by the naval commander and the two High Priests of Ptah [Memphis] together with the king's master-builder [this team made up the post of 'architect' like the medieval bishop/mason system]. He did this in order that I might be his revered one. There was issued a command of the king to the Chief of Works of the King to make it; a tomb of . . . cubits in its length, by 50 cubits in its width by . . . cubits in its height.

The tremendous legacy left by the Fourth Dynasty kings, the definition and memorialization of the basic structure of the ancient Egyptian state, could hold absolute sway only as long as the king was held in absolute awe by his subjects. Perhaps it was the decline of the annual floods and, with them, the national prosperity during the later Old Kingdom that demonstrated that this state of affairs was, ultimately, unsupportable: whatever the reasons, the dynamic of the state changed subtly: the single-minded concentration on the Fourth Dynasty monuments at Giza was not continued in the monuments of their successors. Once established, this new society began to live rather less in the single shadow of the kings who themselves came down from Mount Olympus to join a society that, although it was firmly organized along the lines of the state that had been outlined in stone on the Plateau of Giza, was more wordly wise and less enthusiastic about making such mighty pyramids as their predecessors had done.

This change finds great expression in the arts and architecture. Though enduring in their ruin, the royal pyramids of the Fifth and Sixth Dynasties are not monuments built by the entire nation but by gangs of professional masons and quarrymen working in far smaller numbers than the Giza pyramids required. The sculpture, too, looses the grand fire of the Fourth Dynasty pieces and now, we feel, we are looking at people, at individuals, not at aspects of the royal power. The nobles' tombs became more thoughtful in their appointments, less like a grand logistical exercise and more like a house for a dead person. The false doors – originally simple niches on the outside of the tombs' structure – became deeper and deeper as more pictures and texts were added. Eventually they were so enlarged that they formed rooms and corridors inside the once-solid rectangular tombs. Courtyards, once built as small chapels by the side of the tomb, were also incorporated into the internal apartments and provisions were made for other members of the family. Sculptures of wives, children and servants were placed in the serdabs along with those of the owner of the tomb.

So great is this change in the nobles' tombs – the apparently increasing humanity prevailing at the expense of the qualities of almost non-human

*The recently discovered tomb of two nobles of the Fifth Dynasty
at Sakkara*

absolutism of the Fourth Dynasty monuments – that it has been seen as a
sort of 'Magna Carta' progression, the nobles taking some of the royal
power to themselves. But this is a modern vision about which there is no
general agreement. What some scholars, mainly from the New World,
might characterize as a process of 'humanization' others, in a more European tradition, would describe as a process of lessening 'spirituality' – the
Fourth Dynasty monuments being virtually prayers in stone, the later
sculptures and reliefs being merely fine sculptures of people. In truth, we
know virtually nothing about the psychology of the Fourth Dynasty
people, and not much more about those of later dynasties, much as we
may wish to read notions of 'human nature' into their situation. What we

may find, however, is some understanding of the social codes and relationships of the time.

Despite these problems, however, it is certain that it was the Fourth Dynasty and its monuments that were the bedrock on which the later civilization was built. Without these simple but powerful statements of that early age, the arts of later periods, some of which were times of stress or anarchy, would have lacked coherence and had no strong point of reference. Moreover, adherence to these early standards was quite conscious: every time there was a revival of national prosperity after economic and social collapse, there was also a conscious revival of the old forms of art and architecture. The monuments of Giza became a canon for the later societies of ancient Egypt in the same way that the Doric temple has affected much of our Western architecture.

There is, of course, one great exception to this analogy. Modern society has abandoned the religion of the Greeks and has carried only the form of the ancient temples, elaborated, distorted and decorated, through the ages. (Though it may be observed that classical forms are often used by architects wishing to invoke 'classical' principles of reason and learning.) But while later Egyptians elaborated and decorated the forms of the Giza monuments they also retained the religious and social structures that the architecture of Giza had embodied. The continuity was total. In conjunction with the canons of representational art, formulated during the first three dynasties, Giza furnished the architectural setting for the arts, the government and the religion.

It is, perhaps, in the extraordinary series of private tombs built after the Fourth Dynasty that, more than anywhere else, we may experience the first flowers of these basic forms of architecture and art. All around the cemeteries at Giza and the later royal pyramids, were built cemeteries of nobles' tombs, many of which had rooms filled with reliefs and, sometimes, sculptures. These monuments are the major part of what the Old Kingdom has left us, and they represent a cool view of the ancient world: how its nobles wished to appear in the eye of eternity. Once again, the monuments deal with social relationships rather than with individual personalities.

The tomb of Mereruka at Sakkara is a splendidly mature example of just such a tomb, and one that has not been greatly damaged by stone-plunderers as have so many of these monuments. It is built close to the now-ruined pyramid of King Teti, of the Sixth Dynasty, who was Mereruka's brother-in-law. In the huge rectangular tomb, a warren of rooms contains chapels dedicated to Mereruka's wife and his son Meri-teti. It is to the father's spirit, however, that the main facilities of the tomb are directed. The chapels and rooms that held the equipment and the

The central offering chamber in the tomb of Mereruka at Sakkara

offerings of Mereruka's mortuary cult are filled with wall reliefs – scenes that show endless processions of people bringing offerings to the tomb and scenes of ancient life. The scale of the work is small and intimate, the figures are like those on a television screen or in a weekly magazine, and the fascination of these scenes is fed by an incredible accumulation of detail. Here the carpenters are sawing a plank of wood (what a strange saw and vice!); there they are slaughtering a bull (seems like hard work!); over there they are collecting the taxes (see how they beat the peasants!); and further on they are hunting, herding, harvesting, sowing, and thrashing – all simple rural activities that divert modern visitors from around the world when they visit the ancient monuments. Here the eye of the ancient artist is fixed steadily on his fellow man and he views him with compassion and humour. He shows us his delight in the minutiae of his society and there is a great feeling of satisfaction about the world these ancient people created. They knew that they were on to a good thing.

In Mereruka's tomb the false door was placed right at its heart, directly above the burial chamber which was deep under the ground cut in a large chamber in the underlying limestone. And, giving wonderfully concrete expression to the 'looking glass' qualities of false doors there is a superb colossal figure of Mereruka standing at the centre of this false door, joining the world of the burial chamber beneath to the land of the living above. Here his mortuary priests would leave offerings on the alabaster slab, shaped like a loaf of bread, which still stands at the top of a short flight of steps at the feet of the great statue. Two rows of columns stand in front of the false door and focus the space of the large chamber around the altar-like slab of the offering table. Set into the floor at the centre of the room is a huge stone ring to which bulls were tethered, to be slaughtered and offered to the spirit of Mereruka.

You can see pictures of the bulls being slaughtered on the walls of the offering chamber; one man ties the animal's legs, another cuts its throat with a curved knife while another catches its blood in a bowl. This is followed by scenes that show the butchering – doubtless, with Mereruka's spirit being awarded the best cuts. And after the dead lord had had his spiritual fill of the fresh offerings, they would be taken from the chapel to be eaten by the mortuary priests. These priests, the controllers of the mortuary foundations that were supported by estates throughout the land, did quite well for themselves, like the inmates of a non-celibate monastery. And the spirit of Mereruka, maintained by their prayers and the offices of the cult, continued to spread his energies and powers throughout the land and the skills and the high position that he had enjoyed in life would

Reliefs of herdsmen and their animals – the 'contributions of the villages of the North and South' – that stand before the 'false door' in the chapel of Ptah-hotep, a noble of the Fifth Dynasty. It is probably the work of a sculptor named Ni-ankh-ptah

continue for ever. The system of redistributing the offerings in the tomb chapels and temples not only supported large numbers of priests and administrators but later became a major device of revenue collection from the Egyptian farms.

The tombs also had arrangements in them for the times when the mortuary foundations no longer produced the offerings for the tomb and when the cult of the dead man had finished. In the burial chambers and in rooms that contained the offering tables and the false doors, scenes of the dead receiving their offerings, piled on tables that stand before them, were cut into the walls. Figures of the servants and overseers from the mortuary estates, who bring representations of their usual offerings to the tomb are carved onto the walls of chamber after chamber. Lengthy lists tell of the amounts of this spiritual provender and most begin with the traditional formula:

> An offering which the king gives [as the overseer of prosperity and good order in the land], a thousand of bread, a thousand of beer, a thousand of ointment jars and clothing, a thousand of everything good.

It is an ancient Egyptian survival kit, a self-contained eternity machine for the benefit of those buried under the chapel.

Some of the finest reliefs of Mereruka's tomb are in the central offering hall and show the great nobleman in his robes of office: Mereruka as minister and major factotem of Egypt. Touchingly, he is also shown in his old age supported by two of his sons – though his effigy, as befits a representation designed for all eternity, shows him as a normal Egyptian figure drawing, ageless and without stress or strain, like the columns of the great temples.

The subject matter of these tomb reliefs fall into three basic categories. There are those concerned with the upkeep of the cult at the tomb, such as the slaughtering scenes and the rows of offerers all walking in the direction of the false doors and looking exactly like the present-day procession of Upper Egyptian country people as they carry their goods to market. There are those that show the tomb owner and his family living the noble life and performing the offices of administration of the country: gathering taxes, hunting, and, in series of reliefs that complement the offering scenes, the tomb owner supervising some of the activities of farm life that continued around the year. And finally, there are those that deal exclusively with the ritual events of the next world and show the tomb owner beside his offering tables or in the company of the gods.

In some senses, of course, all these tomb reliefs are of the next world. When Mereruka is seen hunting on the walls of his tomb he hunts in the 'field of reeds' and the animals he kills are the demons he must overcome in the battles of the next world. When Mereruka oversees the activities of farming it is his spiritual power – as one joined with Osiris, the God of the

Underworld and of Fertility – that will help the crops to sprout and grow, just as it is his magical presence in the reliefs that enables him to indicate to his bird trappers the exact moment when they should shut the clap-nets into which the wild birds have been lured – a tricky operation even with divine help. It is these, and similar skills that the dead oversaw for the living workers and it is also a part of what is shown on the walls of Mereruka's tomb.

These tomb scenes, then, are not just simple-minded representations of the nobles' lives as they were lived on earth, based on the religious principle of 'you *can* take it with you!' For example, there is only a fraction of the farming activities that, from archeological investigations we know took place in ancient times; and those that are shown in the tombs are always the same. The crops, too, are always limited to the same varieties, and are but a small selection of what were actually cultivated. The animals depicted are equally limited and are usually shown in exactly the same situations. Understandably, perhaps, it is the exceptions, the rare scenes that show different animals or strange activities that have become the modern favourites. And this is not only because they represent a change from the normal iconography but because the unusual subject matter of these scenes often show a freshness of observation and an especial care about their workmanship. Gathered together in books or museum collections, these often give the false impression that these tombs are filled with a three-ring circus of odd happenings and picturesque events. Our modern predilection for novelty and the unusual blinds us to the old Egyptian virtues which, in these reliefs, are found in the excellence of the drawing and modelling in the more usual subjects of tomb decoration: the desire to do things in the right way and to do them as well as they can possibly be done. It is in the usual scenes of hunting, offering and farming, as well as the drawing of the hieroglyphs and of the owner of the tomb that we will find the mainstream of ancient Egyptian aspirations, not in the occasional cartoons of peasant life.

Even within the limitations of the subject matter of the wall scenes it should not be imagined that the tomb's artists gave a documentary account of ancient life. For, the reliefs contain only the typical – the ideal – vision of the subject as, of course, did most of the world's art before the camera enabled us to see images that existed in split seconds of time. And so used have we become to this portrayal of things *in time* that, for us, even the typical, iconic poses of the Egyptian tombs – which are merely hieroglyphs of activity – may easily be invested, quite falsely, with the quality of time and the drama of a single event. One of the ancient artists boasted:

> I was an artist skilled in my art . . . I knew the movements of the image of man and the carriage of a woman . . . the posing of the arm to bring the hippopotamus low and the movements of a runner.

As, here, the artist generalizes about the actions of hunters, the poses of women, so in Mereruka's tomb it is not a *particular* bull that is being slaughtered but *all* bulls; not a *single* group of slaughterers but *all* slaughterers. And the remarks that these figures make as they work, carved in hieroglyphs above their heads, are the typical remarks of the trade – clichés, the normal, the regular.

Freed by their conventions from the preoccupation of inventing fresh poses and compositions, the Egyptian artists were able to concentrate their skills with all the intensities of Byzantine icon painters. So their finest reliefs have the qualities of meditation, of an exactitude of line and shape, and a subtlety of modelling so intense that new forms may be discovered in the Egyptian reliefs as one might discover them on the human figure. By copying the poses and compositions of their forefathers' work the Egyptian artist gave himself a freedom to concentrate on investing these old images with special qualities of being. In the finest work, every part has an intense quality of life. Like the icons of Byzantium, the finest Egyptian works celebrate holiness, but unlike those, the holiness that the Egyptians celebrated was of life itself.

Apart from the social implications of the texts concerning the organization

A fine fragment of painting from the tomb chapel at Meidum of the nobleman Nefermaat of the early Fourth Dynasty. It shows a young addax antelope held by its keeper (Victoria and Albert Museum, London)

of the mortuary foundations, there are only three other documents from Old Kingdom times that give instructions on personal behaviour. Most of these maxims sound suspiciously like the long-formed opinions of self-appointed elders; the air in front of you is prodded by the wagging of imaginary fingers as you read them. The advice of these instructions is usually fairly basic and presupposes a complex social and moral system which the authors have unhesitatingly accepted as the natural order of the world. There is a morality running through the texts which is deeper than their words. In the most part, they tell you only how the wheels of government may be oiled to your advantage. One maxim tells you, for example, that crime does not pay *because* it is against established order which, inevitably, will triumph in the end. The aim of most of these texts, then, is to inform the reader how he might appear to be wise and great, how to be well thought of, how to be judged innocent and not guilty (irrespective of the deed), and to exclude personal emotions and desires from public view.

> If you are one among guests
> At the table of one greater than you,
> Take what he gives as it is set before you;
> Look at what is before you,
> Don't shoot many glances at him,
> Molesting him offends the [spirit]
> Don't speak to him until he summons,
> One does not know what may displease;
> Speak when he has addressed you,
> Then your words will please the heart.

> If a man's son accepts his father's words,
> No plan of his will go wrong.
> Teach your son to be a hearer,
> One who will be valued by the nobles;
> One who guides his speech by what he was told,
> One regarded as a hearer.
> This son excels, his deeds stand out,
> While failure follows him who hears not.
> The wise wakes early to his lasting gain,
> While the fool is hard pressed.

So, when you have listened to your father's words, got up early in the morning and not eaten the largest slice of cake at the office party you will be a person who will walk the Giza Plateau filled with plans to build a great pyramid? Perhaps not. Such advice is, surely, a part of the pantry wisdom of any age when unquestioning officials are required to organize society. But there is another side to these texts. While, for instance, you are advised to

> Conceal your heart, control your mouth,
> Then you will known amongst the officials;
> Be quite exact before your lord,
> Act so that one will say to him: 'He's the son of that one.'

and this for the sake of your career, for the 'company' of Egypt; privately, however, you are advised to

> Follow your heart as long as you live,
> Do no more than is required,
> Do not shorten the time of 'follow-the-heart'
> Trimming its moment offends the [spirit].

But, less this is taken as a description of the Garden of Eden, you are informed that the best thing to do with a wife is to

> Fill her belly, clothe her back,
> Ointment soothes her body.
> Gladden her heart as long as you live,
> She is a fertile field for her lord.

But, whatever you do,

> Do not contend with her in court,
> keep her from power, restrain her –
> Her eye is her storm when she gazes –
> Thus will you make her stay in your house.

And as for other men's women, the sage advises a strict moral path, for reasons both of business and of self preservation:

> A thousand men are turned away from their good:
> a short moment like a dream,
> Then death comes for having known them.
> Poor advice is 'shoot the opponent',
> When one goes to do it the heart rejects it.
> He who fails through lust of them,
> No affair of his can prosper.

Finally, a splendidly Machiavellian piece of practicality:

> If you are a man who leads,
> Listen calmly to the speech of one who pleads;
> Don't stop him from purging his body
> Of that which he planned to tell.
> A man in distress wants to pour out his heart
> More than that his case be won.

About him who stops a plea
One says: 'Why does he reject it?'
Not all one pleads for can be granted,
But a good hearing soothes the heart.

Surely, this is but the sage advice of a figure in a well-established society, one sure of his position and functions. The awful line 'Not all one pleads for can be granted' seems to have all the Kafka-esque associations of a bottomless pit of structured officialdom that might be expected in a state which, having once exploded with titanic displays of national energy, now rests a little on its laurels.

But the great Nile, fed from the African lakes, did not know of all this energy, of all this wisdom that was engendered on its banks and, if recent estimates of annual flooding levels are correct, the diminution of the bounteous flood levels of early Old Kingdom times was already affecting the national economy by Mereruka's day – the period of the compilation of the Instruction Texts. Doubtless the tried and tested administration, now stocked with hereditary offices, had a firm grasp on the land and the people, and still, at that time, there does not seem to have been serious long-term shortages of food but, ominously, tomb and temple reliefs begin to be made that show starving herdsmen and farmers that may have been forced out of arid areas that, previously, had been reached by the annual floods.

It is interesting that the royal pyramids built at the end of the Old Kingdom do not show a lessening of standard or size over their immediate predecessors. But as soon as the economic strength required to support the royal building programme disappears so does the ability to create even the smallest monuments of stone masonry. The royal monopoly of large-scale public works meant that if there were economic pressures on society such national enterprises would disappear not to re-appear until central-ized government was in a position to monopolize the national surpluses once more. So enormous was the labour force required to quarry, transport and erect even the smallest monuments of good quality stone that as soon as the national wealth dropped below a clearly-defined point the shut-down of the royal works programme was virtually instantaneous.

That point was reached after the completion of the splendid pyramid complex of Pepi II at the end of the Sixth Dynasty, recognized as the end of the Old Kingdom. After this reign, with a few half-finished exceptions, almost all stone building stopped in Egypt for more than a hundred years. Now, in an agrarian society such as ancient Egypt, it would be reasonable in times of falling crop yields and economic stress, for the administrators of the royal court to return to their provincial estates to control them more carefully than was necessary during times of plenty. There would also be

Left The rock-cut tomb chapels and causeways of two provincial governors of Aswan during the late Sixth Dynasty ; Mekhu and his son Sabni

Above The figure of another provincial governor, Wer-ir-ni, from his tomb chapel at Sheik Said. This noble, who lived during the late Sixth Dynasty, is shown standing in a frame tent hung with patterned textiles. The scene was made by the sculptor Ptah-khuw

other social factors related to such a dispersion of the officers of the court: dispossessed farmers and peasants would now be moving through the land and stronger local controls would be required. In short, local officials would be forced into taking action directly and independently of the central court. Although, as a linch-pin of their faith, most of these provincial governors still acknowledged a single king of Egypt, at Memphis after the Sixth Dynasty times, monarchs came and went with a rapidity matched only by the later emperors of Rome or the Mameluk rulers of mediaeval Egypt.

After some fifty years of provincial control with nominal loyalty to the Memphite kings, and this during a period of ever-increasing hardships, one of the provincial families of *nomarchs* (ruler of an Egyptian 'county') rebelled and set up as king of Egypt, a claim that, with the exception of southern Upper Egypt, was accepted throughout the country. The Memphite dynasties were finished and the surviving historical records enter a yet more obscure phase. Traditionally, historians have invited us to view this first 'Intermediate Period' as one in which the rising power of the nobility destroyed the king and the state of Egypt. In fact, in their retreat to the provinces, the nobles were actually guarding the culture of Egypt at a time when central government could no longer sustain it with national enterprises. And with the central government unable to provide mortuary monuments for kings or courtiers, the nobles were now buried, as had been their distant predecessors, in the cemeteries of their separate regions. The court artists of Memphis and the masons used to working the hard stones of the royal architecture did not follow them, however, and the nomarchs now relied on the local craftsmen. The monuments that these provincial artists made are a marvellous chaos of tradition and fantasy. They stand in the same relationship to the architecture of the Old Kingdom as does a Byzantine church to a Roman temple.

One of the most delightful of these tombs was made for the nomarch Ankhtifi, who governed the province of Nekhen about forty miles south of Nagada. Other examples of the freebooting style of these particular provincials' tombs are spread thinly throughout southern Upper Egypt. In the course of his career, Ankhtifi first became nomarch of Nekhen, and then nomarch of the next province to the south, Edfu. Control in many such areas had broken down: Anhktifi proudly described how he set up an efficient administration and distributed food to the wretched inhabitants of the area that he had conquered. Much is made of the provincial battles during those unsettled times, but it is very likely that they were only small affairs; gangs of men from one village boating short distances down the river to fight with the men of the next settlement. Ankhtifi's troops, his 'gallant band' he called them, came from Hefat, his birthplace, that seems to have been no larger than the present-day village of Mo'alla which now occupies that same site. It was to Hefat that Ankhtifi wished to return after his death and he had his tomb cut into a large low-sloped pyramid shaped hill closeby the town. This symmetrical hill, of good white limestone which has been quarried since ancient times, stands at the edge of the cultivated land and is several hundred yards in the front of the cliffs of the *gebel*. From his tomb, Ankhtifi's spirit looks down today on the largely unchanged scene of the blue river, glittering in the sun, bending lazily in its great valley on the way to Luxor and the north.

Although the limestone of Ankhtifi's hill is fine and even-grained, it has faulted severely and the fissures run right through the tomb chapel. This long room is set in the hill like a corridor that runs each side of the entrance doorway. Ankhtifi was to be buried in a chamber that was cut at the bottom of the large pit that stands in the centre of the narrow room. Right through the length of the narrow chapel the quarrymen left two rows of pillars, their positions planned not as regular architecture but dictated by the natural fissures in the limestone. They make a forest of stone and where the shattered rock came away during their work the masons made good with a poorly applied local plaster so that the columns stand like tree trunks, all different shapes and sizes: some round, some octagonal, some square, some a mixture of forms and all tapering towards the ceiling.

The decorations are equally bizarre. The major wall scene that remains –

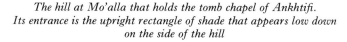

The hill at Mo'alla that holds the tomb chapel of Ankhtifi.
Its entrance is the upright rectangle of shade that appears low down
on the side of the hill

Remains of some of the crazy paintings in Ankhtifi's tomb chapel.
In the upper section three men enthusiastically butcher a black-and-
white spotted cow. Below them a boatload of canoers set off down
the river

one much beloved of political historians who have found on it the name of
an otherwise unknown king in hieroglyphs an inch high – is a painting of
Ankhtifi spearing fishes in a field of reeds that also holds a fine flight of
pin-tailed ducks; beside him, boatloads of tiny rowers rush unheedingly
past: above, a group of slaughterers energetically disembowel an ox. Other
walls show jolly looking rows of offerers bringing produce to the tomb –
not in the manner of the Memphite chapels, in the time-honoured order
of rows of elegant figures each carrying their offerings with them to the
tomb, but on donkeys drawn so carefully that you may almost see the tip
of the artist's tongue poised in concentration, yet so clumsily that some of
the donkeys have gained or lost a leg here or there in the mass of their
procession. But their eyes look at us, alive, from the walls.

It would seem that something of the same spirit of independence which
affected the local nomarchs had also affected their artists, for their pictures
are bold, happy and unapologetically rustic. Ankhtifi's tomb is a carnival

of disorder, of playful colour combinations, and of strange drawings by artists who understood the basic subject matter of their art, but by some disjoined process, perhaps by a complete lack of contact with the earlier work of the Old Kingdom, have not ordered their work in the correct way. Instead, they have left us riotous scenes of country life filled with innovative poses and colour schemes that would have amazed the careful craftsmen of Mereruka's day. They created a style of art which, though entirely dependent on the courtly arts of Memphis for its form, was fresh and quite new. And in this process men like Ankhtifi and the local artists they subsidized, sustained the national culture throughout the worst period of its history.

A figure of Ankhtifi carved on one of the columns in his tomb chapel

CHAPTER EIGHT

INSECURITIES AND EMPIRE

With the return of the nobles to the provinces of Egypt at the end of the Old Kingdom, several towns gained prominence that were later to play important roles in Egyptian history. By far the greatest of these was Thebes, some twenty miles south of Nagada, now the tourist resort of Luxor. There had been a town of some size at the site since the Archaic Period and there had also been extensive settlements in the area for a long time before that, but this ancient city slips out of the archeological record entirely during the Old Kingdom when the power of the land was focused around the royal court of Memphis. At the end of that period, however, tombs of local dignitaries were again made in the hills that face Thebes from across the river. Later, both this western city of the dead and the eastern city of the living came to hold the finest tombs and temples of the country. Thebes, whose riches were legend in the ancient world – Homer's 'hundred-gated' Thebes – became the capital of Egypt and the seat of an empire that stretched right through the ancient Near East.

How did this dramatic change of national outlook take place: that such a traditional inward-looking people was stimulated to found a great empire built on continuous foreign campaigns? There are very few military scenes in the tombs and temples before the Sixth Dynasty and there is nothing about war or its 'splendours' in Old Kingdom literature. It appears that this national transformation was the result of contacts with other nations and the contradictions to the traditional Egyptian world-view that these contacts provoked.

The crop failures that had precipitated the end of the Old Kingdom were, it seems, caused by erratic short-term phenomena – sharp variations of annual flood levels that created deep economic instability. Then, after a hundred and twenty years of minor kings and petty kingdoms, the princes of Thebes, who had long been independent of the squabbling northern monarchies, declared war on the rest of Egypt and began to fight their way down the Nile Valley as their ancient ancestors had at the

Colossal Osiride statues of King Ramesses II in his mortuary temple at Thebes

115

end of the Predynastic Period. Ankhtifi, perhaps the northern kings' most southern ally, might have been an early victim of this long march north and, indeed, may never have enjoyed burial in his splendid tomb at Mo'alla. Thus, after some political to-ing and fro-ing, the Middle Kingdom was established by these southern kings, a period of such finesse in its art and literature that many consider it to have been the 'classical' age of ancient Egypt. And at this time there was a dramatic succession of very high Niles which flooded land that had not seen water for generations. These floods and irrigation projects that were undertaken in Middle Egypt all helped to revive the national economy.

The first of these southern kings had made their base at Thebes but their descendents, the monarchs of the Twelfth Dynasty, moved the capital to the north as the Predynastic kings had done before them. These kings revived the old Memphite stone-working traditions, all the precise skills that had been the hallmark of Old Kingdom work. Indeed, under these new kings the state arts were further refined until they were more ordered and more elegant than the works of their predecessors. Surviving royal jewellery shows minor arts of equally magnificence and fragments of the architecture – the buildings themselves are mostly destroyed – are also precise and jewel-like. The Middle Kingdom was a near three-hundred-year period of revival and refinement.

But this glittering monarchy and its apparently stable administration did not survive for very long. As befitted kings whose predecessors had taken Egypt by force of arms and had seen the ruin of all the earlier royal funerary monuments of Egypt, they were far less optimistic about their eventual fates than their Old Kingdom predecessors. A text, supposedly written by a dead king for the instruction of his son, describes his murder by the night guards of his own palace and advises his son to sleep with sword by his side. Under the stone shells of their pyramids, the corridors and chambers twist and turn in an effort to foil the plunderers who would eventually attack their tombs.

No one knows the reasons why this brittle kingdom finally failed. Traditionally it has been ascribed to continued political machinations; dynastic struggles within the royal family and the refusal of the nomarchs to relinquish their power to the centralized royal administration. More recent suggestions have included the theory that the same high flood levels that first brought the increased level of national prosperity may, by continuing at even higher levels, brought disorder and destruction to the farmlands. The failure of the state at the end of the Twelfth Dynasty is dramatically underlined by the lack of large standing monuments from that time and the period that followed. Not that this by itself is necessarily an indication that life in Egypt was now chaotic or that the splendours of the court had completely disappeared, merely that the state resources and the power of the king were no longer sufficient to support the enormous

A small shrine made at Karnak during the reign of Senusert I of the Middle Kingdom

manpower required for quarrying building stone and erecting substantial monuments.

So far as is known, it seems that the economic structure of the Old and Middle Kingdoms had developed along very particular lines. The huge public works projects of the royal pyramids and the elaborate endowments of the mortuary cults had led to the establishment of a skilled, hereditary bureaucracy of priests, government officials and estate managers. The great temples, which had been granted privileges similar to the mortuary foundations, also controlled large estates and huge labour forces that were a sort of national treasury. The bureaucracy was large, efficient and well

117

organized, a system that allowed for easy expansion. The great estates incoporated large numbers of non-Egyptians into their service, as did the royal court: biblical stories of various dates tell how men like Moses and Joseph thrived at high levels in the Egyptian administration. Lower down in the social scale, one group had brought their families into Egypt from Nubia and served first as mercenaries and, later, as a special administrative police. And at a non-bureaucratic level many groups of nomads annually brought their herds of sheep to graze in the Eastern Delta. Significantly, several popular stories of Middle Kingdom date were set partially in other countries; here too we may see the traditional narrow vision of the Egyptians slowly widening. At this same time there were contacts with other countries on a much wider scale than ever before – either by trade and diplomacy, as with the Lebanon and Syria, or by conquest and military settlement, as in Nubia and the Sudan.

So, when the centralized economy collapsed at the end of the Twelfth Dynasty and the administration of the land was once more conducted at provincial levels, there were large numbers of non-Egyptians in the country, working in all layers of the administration. The number was greatly increased when population pressures far to the north of Egypt forced the semi-nomadic tribes of those areas into Syria and Lebanon and, eventually, into the Eastern Delta where, at first, they settled into the deserted towns of earlier Egyptian colonies.

As more and more of these tribesmen came into Egypt, not fighting battles or even having to pass through occupied border posts, there was no one power in the land that appreciated the extent of this infiltration. Similar migrations in later Egyptian history were quickly apprehended by the administration of Ramesses III, of the Nineteenth Dynasty, which, in confrontations and set battles around the country, killed large numbers of tribesmen who were attempting to colonize the Delta, in league, apparently, with insurgent foreign mercenaries who had long served in the Egyptian armies. But during the Second Intermediate Period such a prompt and devastating response was not possible.

With the great advantage of hindsight, later traditions of Egyptian history tell a different story of these infiltrations. For example, Manetho, the ancient historian, claimed that

> For what cause I know not, a blast of God smote us, and unexpectedly, from the regions of the East, invaders of obscure race marched in confidence of victory against our land. By main force they easily seized it without striking a blow; and having overpowered the rulers of the land, they burnt our cities ruthlessly, razed to the ground the temples of the gods, and treated all the natives with a cruel hostility, massacring some and leading into slavery the wives and children of others.

Manetho goes on to tell a tough tale of foreign invasion and conquest that, once again, culminated in an army of Upper Egyptians reconquering the country and, finally, expelling the barbarians.

Now, although historians are always pleased to observe that the ancient temple priest was correct in his simple historical account, they are equally happy, when they believe him to be wrong, to claim that he was merely repeating old folk tales or morsels of ancient propaganda. And in the case of the 'Hyksos' – as these foreign pharaohs are called – there are great differences of opinion, especially concerning the identity of these mysterious kings. It is possible that they were actually the sons of Middle Eastern princes who had been sent to the Egyptian court in friendship and who had been close to the throne for generations; also that it was these foreign nobles who took the throne of Egypt with the help of some of the nomarchs. What relationship this foreign elite shared with the nomadic infiltrators of Egypt is not yet known. Other historians, denying the existence of these two separate groups, identify the foreigners as a single entity, the southernmost part of racial migrations that were then taking place throughout the entire Middle East. Romantics have suggested that it was another arm of these great migrations that is represented as the Greek armies at the seige of Troy. Somewhat less romantically, modern attitudes to migrants have undoubtedly coloured many explanations of the meagre source material. Of a later episode involving foreigners in Egypt, one historian has written:

> Amongst them [the conspirators] were a Lybian, a Lycian, a Syrian . . . and another foreigner, Kedendenna by name, of uncertain nationality. The unhealthy character of the conditions at the court . . . are thus patent. Foreign stewards and butlers, whose fidelity is purchased, are now the reliance of the Pharaoh.

More recently, another historian has asserted that the ancient Egyptians were a black race and that the Hyksos were white invaders of 'indescribable barbarism'.

One thing is sure, it was the 'foreignness' of these people that was seized upon by the Theban princes (who had in fact been living in peace with these neighbours in the north of the country for some time) as the excuse to march up through Egypt once again, this time conquering the country in the name of nationalism to break the foreign yoke. With the return of agricultural prosperity, which in itself, may well have been a precondition from the beginning of these Theban wars of liberation – Egypt regained its autonomy and once again the nation thrived.

--- ◆ • ◆ • ◆ ---

On a fine stela that commemorated the expulsion of the foreign kings, the Theban warlord and founder of the New Kingdom, Ahmose, records the text of a letter, sent to a Nubian chieften from the Hyksos king, in which the Nubians are encouraged to attack Thebes from the south while the Theban armies were fighting the Hyksos in the north.

> Come, fare north at once, do not be timid. See, he [the Theban war lord] is here with me . . . I will not let him go until you have arrived. Then we will divide the towns of this Egypt between us.

Here, according to the Theban scribes, the devilish Hyksos were proposing that their southern neighbours should open a second front and that, after victory was attained, the two armies would divide Egypt between them. As the Thebans campaigned in the north they must have looked nervously over their shoulders towards Thebes and the south. But the borders held and the Nubians did not come to the aid of the Hyksos.

Although it is not yet proven that it was the Hyksos who introduced many mechanical innovations into Egypt, it is nevertheless true that it was during their rule or the period shortly thereafter, that many did appear in the Nile Valley for the first time. A whole new weapon technology had been developed in countries to the north, and Egypt quickly adopted the new short sword, the chariot and the horse; the *shaduf*, a simple but highly effective device for raising water, brought with it the possibility of a second and third annual crop to parts of the Egyptian farmland. These and other machines showed what advances were taking place in other countries.

With a freshly victorious army, a new set of weapons and the realization that Egypt was vulnerable to invasion from other countries, it is not altogether surprising that the kings of Egypt should turn their attentions to foreign wars and the founding of empires. National feelings of insecurity were answered by empire-building and, for the rest of its history Egypt was caught up in imperial wars, the maintenance of vassal states and, finally, the defence of its homeland. Thus a three-hundred-year period was initiated that was filled with the 'glorious exploits' that are often enthusiastically recounted by egyptologists in an attempt to enhance the rather dusty image of ancient Egypt. Terms borrowed from the histories of other empires are often used to describe the deeds of the ancient kings. The New Kingdom pharaohs have, for example, been dubbed with titles such as 'the Napoleon of ancient Egypt', 'the Magnificent', 'the Great'. Unfortunately, this has created a seductive *Boy's Own Paper* world that is a far cry from the ancient reality.

Nevertheless, it is difficult not to feel that during this period a life of oriental magnificence arose and flourished in the rarified atmosphere of an imperial court. For the first time in Egyptian history, many kings spent considerable time outside Egypt leaving the administration of the country in the hands of officials who commemorated themselves and their positions in their splendid tomb chapels at Thebes. When the kings were in Egypt they lived in vast palaces built either at the edge of the desert or in the lush

Delta – both areas somewhat removed from the centre of Egyptian life. The warrior pharaohs gave enormous donations of war booty, even entire foreign cities to the temple foundations and it was during this period that gigantic temples were built at Thebes. The achievement is still impressive, the temples large, lavish and luxuriant.

The best preserved temple of the New Kingdom is one built at Medinet Habu by Ramesses III on the west bank at Thebes. This was the last of the great royal mortuary temples to be completed, and because these monuments were often made partly from the stone of their predecessor's temples, it has survived relatively undamaged. Over a period of some four centuries many temples were built for the mortuary cults of the New

Battle reliefs of Seti I at Karnak showing the king fighting in Libya and Palestine

Kingdom monarchs who, together with their successors, were buried in the Valley of the Kings, a desert *wadi* that lies behind the western Theban cliffs. As well as ministering to the cults of the dead rulers, the temple enclosures were also centres of the royal administration during the kings' lifetimes, containing offices, archives, storerooms, and living quarters for large numbers of officials. Some of the temples had palaces attached to them: Ramesses III's even had quarters for his harem, and shows reliefs of him with some of his concubines, who at that time included large numbers of the daughters of foreign princes. The reliefs were carved on the walls of a four-square pavilion that also formed the entrance to the mortuary temple complex. It is an unusual building for Egypt, its international appearance deriving from the fortresses of Syria and the Lebanon.

The temple complex of Medinet Habu

*The East Gate and pavilion of the temple of Ramesses III at
Medinet Habu*

It had been Ramesses III who, in the earlier half of his reign, had fought
foreign armies and rebellious mercenary soldiers who had intended to
bring their tribes to settle in Egypt. Fighting them on the land and at sea
he had won the last major Egyptian victory for a thousand years. Scenes
from the campaigns cover the walls of the outer sections of Ramesses III's
temple, which was built in the centre of a huge royal compound: a model
of the Egyptian state.

This great stone temple consisted of a series of courts, each smaller than
the last and, as you penetrated the centre of the building towards the
sanctuary of the god, the floors rose and the ceilings were made lower and
lower. Like all Egyptian temples it is a model of their universe; the stone
roof is painted a fine blue and decorated with yellow stars – the Egyptian
night sky; the pillars are carved in plant forms that make a monumental
field of reeds that you must pass through to reach the creation mound at
the temple's heart – the sanctuary of the god, Amun-Re. On his statue the
priests would perform the same daily rituals as they did on the Amun-Re
of the great temple of Karnak and, indeed, on the gods of the other temples
of Egypt. Annually, the Amun-Re of the temple of Ramesses III would be
visited by the Amun-Re of the temple of Karnak across the river, which
was periodically taken in festal procession to several of the other Theban
temples.

Around the central sanctuary were rooms that housed the precious

The central axis of the temple of Ramesses III at Medinet Habu

objects used in the ceremonial of the temple rites. These had been donated in large amounts by Ramesses III who had made similar gifts to many of the other temples of Egypt. As well as the cult chambers there were statue rooms record offices, temple 'treasuries', a slaughtering room for bulls, and chapels for other gods, including an open-roof chapel built for the sun god Re. Between these inner suites and the outer portions of the temple was a pillared hall. The larger and more public courts, which unlike the inner areas did not require ritual cleanliness for admission, were not carved with the religious scenes of the cult rooms but with the records of Ramesses' more secular activities, his battles, and his great lion and bull hunts. In the outermost courtyard of the temple Ramesses III would appear in person to his courtiers, walking onto a wooden platform that was set into a wall of the court. The martial decorations around this

Columns in the second court of the mortuary temple of Ramesses III

Details of the architectural decorations in the first court of
Ramesses III's mortuary temple

'doorway of appearance' were so composed that when the figure of the king emerged from his palace he looked larger than life, a clever illusion that depended on the careful control of the overall decorative scheme in the courtyard. Another illusion in the compound that strove for the effect of grandeur is contained in the entrance pavilion, where it seems that the height of the architectural elements have been deliberately composed in a false perspective to make the deep-set entrance doorway appear even deeper than it really is. This device is similar to that employed by Bernini in his design for the Scala Regia of the Vatican Apartments, in the seventeenth century.

The south side of Ramesses III's mortuary temple. The long sunlit wall is covered with the lists of the temple calendar. In the foreground are the remains of the king's palace

Ramesses walked to his 'doorway of appearance' through the vaulted halls of his throne-room. Though to modern eyes this palace may appear quite modest for an ancient emperor, by the tastes of the day it was a lavish building: ancient Egyptians usually inhabited small houses made almost entirely of mud brick with flat roofs. Behind this vaulted audience chamber, where the royal throne stood on an alabaster dais – a grander version of the usual provisions in many Egyptian households – lay a private suite of apartments where Ramesses had a bedroom and bathroom. From these rooms a narrow corridor enabled Ramesses to visit other similar rooms built for his queens and other members of his harem. These modest apartments, all carefully designed and well-laid out, could only be entered by one easily guarded doorway.

To the side of the palace lay a garden with a well that was provided with a fine stone stairway that led down to the water table. The water was used not only for the royal garden but also for the ceremonials of the temple cult. Describing the well in a temple inventory, a scribe said that Ramesses III had brought Nun, the primeval water, to the temple. As he walked in his garden, Ramesses III would have seen a part of the great temple calendar which, copied from an earlier version in another temple, had been carved right down one side of the temple. Listed in great detail in this enormous register were all the requirements of the feasts that were celebrated there – thousands upon thousands of offerings, from cabbages and bulls to gold and silver bullion. The greater part of these offerings was food, and it was this that provided the most vital medium between men and ancient gods.

The maintenance of this huge programme of annual rituals and festivals throughout the twenty-four years of Ramesses III's reign was entrusted, as it had been by his predecessors in their temples, to the governors and chamberlains of the court who had their quarters on the side of the temple opposite the palace. Here were all the offices of government, the archives, apartments for the scribes, royal stables, and large numbers of storerooms for all kinds of produce. In the reign of Ramesses III there were no less than 86,486 people controlled by the bureaucracies of the Theban temple estates, which were at that time the major religious institutions of Egypt being some four times larger than those of the other temples. It was a huge conglomerate which operated more than 400,000 head of cattle in estates of some 143,000 acres spread throughout the land. This complex also controlled a large fleet of boats and numerous workshops; it also owned fifty-six towns in Egypt and nine foreign cities.

As one would expect, the temple revenues were immense and, as well as these, Ramesses also made continual donations of produce, large amounts of gold, silver, copper, and richly furnished trappings to enrich the temple cult. The king made similar donations to the other temples of Egypt. The temple foundations held one fifth of the farmland in Egypt and actually owned some five per cent of the population, which was held in direct bondage.

It was an extraordinary system of royal patronage, and one listed in great detail for the entire reign of Ramesses III on a single papyrus. This, with its detailed accounting of his work for the gods was apparently designed to smooth the passage of the king in the next world. One hundred and thirty feet in length, compiled by four different scribes, this document lists the property of the largest temple foundations of Egypt and Ramesses' donations to them. The accounts of many of the smaller temples were not included, so the total amount of property owned by the temples was considerably greater than indicated by the papyrus.

Clearly, the temple estates were a major part of the national economy, and the continual royal donations were a concrete expression of the surpluses of the national wealth. According to the papyrus, the Ramesses III compound at Medinet Habu alone, controlled some 62,626 people, including the farm workers and supervisors who supplied the temple with produce from all over Egypt for the great feasts and a considerable body of resident controllers and government officials.

Now, so remote is this situation from our modern experience that it is difficult to appreciate how such a system of government might function – but function it did, and for a very long time; it is an elaborate structure of state enterprise conducted in an economy that operated without money or money-substitutes. Any surpluses in the economy, either of goods and materials, or the labour that these products could support, were given to the gods which had initially granted this bounty. Usually, large numbers of artists and masons were accommodated inside the Egyptian state, whose work, though economically 'non-productive' in the modern sense, was regarded by the Egyptians as the core of their nation. The surplus wealth of the nation, expressed as art and architecture, was donated by the kings to the gods. One such donation, to the cult statue of Re in the great temple of Heliopolis, is described in Ramesses' papyrus:

> I made for thee [i.e. Ramesses III made for Re] august amulets of fine gold, with inlay of real lapis lazuli and real malachite. I attached them to thy body in the great house of thy protection and thy magnificence, in thy splendid seat, that they might protect the august limbs as perennial amulets for thy great, grand and lovely form.

As well as these small donations, which are listed in their hundreds in the papyrus, Ramesses endowed his principal temple at Medinet Habu and many other smaller shrines and temples throughout the land:

> I built a house for thy son, Khonsu in Thebes, of good sandstone, red quartzite and black granite. I overlaid its doorposts and doors with gold, with inlay-figures of electrum [a gold-silver alloy], like the horizon of heaven. I worked

upon thy statues in the gold-houses, with every splendid costly stone which my hands brought.

The equivalent description of the great Medinet Habu temple in the papyrus, which sounds like a passage from the 'Book of a Thousand and One Nights', is some forty times longer.

Despite the experience of the Hyksos, there were still large numbers of foreign officials at the court of Ramesses III, a fact that should surely be taken to mean that this was a quite normal aspect of Egyptian life. In 1166

Above *The temple of Khonsu at Karnak, built during the Nineteenth and Twentieth Dynasties*

Right *Part of the ruined mortuary temple of Ramesses II, called the Ramesseum*

B.C. some of these officials, in league with a queen and a number of royal concubines conspired to kill the old king and after a reign of thirty-one years Ramesses was, it seems, a victim of a harem conspiracy. Parts of the records of the trials of those implicated in Ramesses' murder – proceedings overseen by the spirit of the dead king – describe those implicated in a minor degree as being sentenced to mutilation, while those directly accused of the plot were either invited to commit suicide or suffered a regicide's fate of impaling. At this point it is difficult not to see parallels between this court and those of the monarchs of the past five hundred years, in both East and West. There is, however, one essential difference between these more modern cultures and those of ancient Egypt – one characteristic that sets ancient Egypt apart – the absence, almost, of any personalities in ancient history and of a complete lack of a royal personality cult. The full irony of this is epitomized by the fact that, in common with most New Kingdom monarchs, Ramesses III's mummy has been preserved to this day – we may look at the very flesh and bones of the old man, yet still we may not begin to put thoughts back into his dried-out skull.

–•◆•–

> I met a traveller from an antique land
> Who said: Two vast and trunkless legs of stone
> Stand in the desert . . . Near them, on the sand,
> Half sunk, a shattered visage lies, whose frown,
> And wrinkled lip, and sneer of cold command,
> Tell that its sculptor well those passions read
> Which yet survive, stamped on these lifeless things,
> The hand that mocked them, and the heart that fed:
> And on the pedestal these words appear:
> 'My name is Ozymandias, king of kings:
> Look on my works, ye Mighty, and despair!'
> Nothing besides remains. Round the decay
> Of that colossal wreck, boundless and bare
> The lone and level sands stretch far away.

Shelley's fine image of imperial decay was made when another emperor, Napoleon, was fresh in the English consciousness. And even now the ancient kings only 'live' by such assimilations of character, or as myths made by historians. Their personalities are still mysterious, elusive and, perhaps, never amenable to modern sympathies. For, though mortal, they were also gods. We deal with kings who seldom bothered to record details of their individuality on the monuments and the few exceptions to this

The base of a colossal statue of Ramesses II in the Temple of Luxor

rule are so rare that, in their isolation, they do not allow us to build a personality from them. We have no basic frame of reference in which to place such solitary facts. It has been suggested that to avoid being merely an incoherent cluster of notes, all musical melodies are essentially variations on earlier themes: in a similar manner our understanding of the past is based on the themes of previous interpreters and this, inevitably tells us as much about the singer as it does about the song.

The name of Shelley's king, Ozymandias is a Greek corruption of a part of the name of Ramesses II, who died in 1237 B.C., some forty years before Ramesses III came to the throne. He too had been a warrior in his youth and was a prolific builder of monuments and temples. In consequence he was christened 'Ramesses the Great' by nineteenth-century historians. The beautiful ruin of his mortuary temple, today called the Ramesseum, is still a favourite among visitors to Thebes and was in part copied by Ramesses III in his temple at Medinet Habu, which is largely a flatulent version of this vibrant original. The ancient Greeks identified this picturesque ruin as the palace of Memnon, the legendary King of Ethiopia, son of Eos the Goddess of the Dawn. Memnon had fought at Troy, where he had killed the Greek Antilochus before meeting his death at the hands of vengeful Achilles. His Theban palace, known as the Memnonium, was one of the main attractions of the city of Thebes and much visited by ancient Greek and Roman travellers.

These ancient tourists sought to understand the monuments in terms of their own knowledge and experience – just as today's guide books, giving brief political and cultural histories, and facts and figures about the monuments, attempt this same duty. So, when we visit the great silent buildings we see them in a modern setting that we have made for ourselves, and similarly, the Greek and Roman visitors of two thousand years ago shaped the Theban landscape according to their quite different preoccupations. Memnon had not only lived in the great temple of Ramesses II, where pictures of battles – the Trojan wars – might have been seen on the walls but he was also buried nearby in the Valley of the Kings in a tomb that is now identified as having jointly belonged to Ramesses V and VI. And in the fields beside Memnon's palace stood a memorial to this fallen hero, one of a pair of statues that we can now identify as colossi of Amenhotep III which mark the position of that king's now-vanished mortuary temple. In 27 B.C. the northernmost of the two stone statues was partly shattered by an earthquake and thereafter at sunrise its stone emitted sounds 'like the twanging of a harp'; this, modern guidebooks tell us, is due to vibrations set up by the rapidly changing humidity and temperature that

Graffiti carved on the foot of the colossus of Memnon, some telling
that the ancient visitors to the site heard the statue utter sounds
at sunrise

commonly occur during the Egyptian dawn. The legs and bases of the twin figures, which stand more than 70 feet high, were engraved with texts by the early tourists expressing wonder at the singing statue and admiration for the mighty Memnon, King Priam's loyal nephew whose death the stone statue daily lamented. It is interesting that so many of the Theban monuments were connected by the Greeks to Memnon – king of Ethiopia, the 'dawn land' – who was, perhaps, a recognition in myth of a part of the roots of their own culture.

A phonetic connection between the name of Memnon and of Ramesses II may have suggested itself to an inquisitive Greek while talking to Egyptian priests about the ancient kings, for the phrase 'Mery-Amun', a common royal epithet meaning 'beloved of Amun', perhaps sounded something like the Greek name Memnon. Mery-Amun was part of the full name of Ramesses II, as was the sonorous name of Shelley's Ozymandias, which was derived from the Egyptian phrase 'User-Maat-Ra'.

Ramesses II's two principal names (our Ramesses again being a Greek version) were 'User-Maat-Ra Setep-en-Re' and 'Ra-messe Mery-Amun' and these were first deciphered from the ancient hieroglyphs by the Frenchman Champollion in 1822, who quickly established the framework of Egyptian history. From the beginning of these studies Ramesses II attracted a good deal of scholarly interest; first, because of the king's high reputation in classical histories and second, because of the large number of splendid monuments that the king had built throughout Egypt and Nubia. Some of these temples carried enormous war reliefs not, as the Greeks had believed, of the battle for Troy, but of battles fought in the Near Eastern empire. One battle in which the king had fought in person, and fought valiantly, was particularly well documented and Ramesses II soon gained the reputation of a hero. When his mummy was found in 1881, in a cache of New Kingdom pharaohs, Ramesses II was seen to have been a tall distinguished man. Now here, indeed, was the stuff of empire!

> To think that once the destinies of the world were ruled, without appeal, by the nod of this head . . . What force of will of passion and colossal pride must once have dwelt therein!

These sentiments of Pierre Loti's must have been prompted, no doubt, by the scholarly translations of Ramesses II's own texts:

> Then His majesty arose like his father Mont [the war god] and took the accoutrements of battle, and girt himself with his corselet: he was like Ba'al in his hour and the great pair of horses which bore his majesty were named 'Victory-in-Thebes'.

This was a king, who, the hieroglyphs proclaimed, had fought the Hittite armies virtually singled handed from his war chariot until reinforcements had arrived on the plain of Kadesh to carry the day for Egypt!

After the battle, in a desperate speech that is reported in detail in the Egyptian accounts, the Hittite king mourns the desolation of his lands and his desertion by the gods; a penalty for fighting with the Egyptian king:

> It were fitting that we be despoiled of all our possessions, my eldest daughter at the head of them, and that we bring gifts of homage to the good god [Ramesses II], so that he may give us peace and we may live.

That Ramesses did, indeed, have mercy on his defeated enemies, we know from the text of the elaborate peace treaty that he concluded with the Hittites, a copy of which is preserved on a wall of the great temple of Amun-Re at Karnak. The daughter of the Hittite king, who had been sent to join Ramesses' harem, as a part of the terms of this treaty, eventually become one of the king's favourites, earning the title of 'great wife', a description that was probably the literal truth for much of the time because during a reign of nearly seventy years Ramesses sired more than a hundred sons.

All in all, it appeared that Ramesses II, the Great, was a king fit for the Victorian history books, someone to think of as you went out to bat to save the match for the school or, indeed, as you led your men over the top at Ypres or Vimy Ridge. Thus, Gaston Maspero, the greatest French scholar of the second half of the last century described the ancient accounts of Ramesses' conduct at the celebrated battle of Kadesh as bearing 'no traces

'Ramasses II defeats the Khetans' – an illustration by Evelyn Paul published in 1914

of the coldness of official reports, and a warlike strain runs through it from one end to the other so as to invest it with life after a lapse of more than thirty centuries'. The ancient scribe, observed Maspero, did not give 'full vent to his enthusiasm until the moment when he describes his hero [Ramesses II] left almost alone, charging the enemy in the sight of his followers'. Even James Breasted, the great American historian of the succeeding generation and a humanist of most careful morality, declared that the main body of the accounts of the battle were written in 'sober and careful prose'.

Tragically, Maspero's younger son, a man destined to follow his father into egyptology with equal honour, died at Vauqois in one of the early phases of the battle for Verdun. After the Great War had finished Breasted reflected on its horrors in his last study of Egyptian religion, *The Dawn of Conscience*. At the same time many new strains of historical judgement were emerging and some showed more moral subtlety and social awareness than the simpler and more confident visions of Maspero and the young Breasted.

Since the Great War, too, further discoveries in Egypt and Boghazköy, the Hittite capital in Anatolia, had changed the whole picture of Ramesses' campaigns from the enthusiastic construction of the older generation. The truth, as it now appears, is that Ramesses II fought inconclusively against the Hittite armies for some fifteen years. The young king's heroic actions at the battle of Kadesh, where he had displayed such personal bravery, were precipitated by a rash advance in front of his main force and Ramesses had to fight for his life when he was isolated. After several protracted campaigns the two nations had signed a peace treaty which succeeded a similar contract drawn up a hundred years before. Although Ramesses II may well have done the best that he could for his nation in the circumstances, these new facts were not sufficient to save his reputation as a hero.

Indeed, Ramesses II's reputation has again been reformed in the light of more recent experience. After totalitarianism had arisen in Europe, Ramesses was no longer seen as a combination of Henry VIII and good Prince Hal, but as Joseph Stalin. In these new assessments the ancient king's reputation suffered not only from the suppressed angers of cold war politics but also, perhaps, from the disillusionment of scholars who could no longer trust simplistic interpretations of the ancient texts: 'The fact remains that the arrogant bellowing of victory comes as an insincere ostentation similar to the bloated bulk of Ramesses II's monuments or to his shameless appropriation of the monuments of his ancestors. Blatant advertising was used to cover up the failure to attain past glories', commented Professor John Wilson in 1951 – a portrait of the king that was

Part of the long text that describes the battle of Kadesh. This version is carved on the outer walls of the Temple of Luxor

recently given a Freudian twist of the knife by Lord Clark with his remark that Ramesses II was certainly a megalomaniac!

So, at the end of the day, what can we actually *know* about these ancient kings? Are not concepts of personality and our modern assessments of it bound to be redundent when we attempt to evaluate men who were gods in their own lifetimes? As for Ramesses' 'dishonesty' and 'megalomania', it would be true to say that merely by virtue of his reigning for so many years there would be more of his monuments surviving than those of most other New Kingdom pharaohs. This would also give Ramesses II's monuments (and not his *personality*!) an elaborate chronology of their own, rich transformations of style not shared by the monuments of short-lived kings. Further, there is not the slightest evidence that Ramesses II's usurpation of the monuments of his predecessors – though possibly appearing dishonest to our eyes – was done in ill will, megalomania or any other mental condition.

But had not this Ramesses sanctioned many of his monuments to be emblazoned with propaganda accounts for the royal victory at Kadesh which now, to many people's great dismay, have turned out to have been something less than the whole truth? If we examine the war texts of other Egyptian kings we will find, with the exception, perhaps, of the description of Ramesses' personal behaviour at Kadesh, virtually the same order of events occurring in the description of every battle. And this is even true of the records of Tuthmosis III, the king who seems to have taken over Ramesses II's reputation as a sober and honest relator of historical events. Moreover, even politicians of this present century have been known to mythologize real situations for their people in times of stress, using rolling prose and fiery rhetoric: soldiers still fight for glory, freedom and honour.

The accounts of the Kadesh battle, then, are neither honest nor dishonest, but simply an attempt on behalf of the throne of Egypt to retain the old values of consistency and world order, the total domination of Pharaoh, while admitting the new realities of their age – the necessity for the king to treat with *equal* monarchs, this a theological impossibility in terms of the Egyptian world order – and finding a place in Middle Eastern society. Perhaps, as history, the Kadesh texts might find a modern parallel in a mixture of a chorus from 'Rule Britannia' and contemporary accounts of the Battle of Britain.

The venerable state ruled over by Ramesses II was founded upon beliefs that were continually being called into question by the changes in Near Eastern society. It was patently obvious, for instance, that individual events (rather than the cyclic events of the calendar) *could* and, indeed, *had* affected the destiny of Egypt for some considerable time and that the state *did* exist in a changing world, in historical time. But this was a truth that could hardly be adapted to the vision of a culture that had built the Giza pyramids and always stressed the overriding importance of cyclic, recurrent events. So Ramesses II's armies had not only to fight the Hittites but also their own belief which would hardly admit that these foreigners were a threat to the sovereign state of Egypt. In the texts that describe these battles it is hardly surprising, therefore, that the enemy is transformed into the forces of darkness and confusion, and that the king of Egypt and his ordered world, inevitably, triumphed.

Throughout the course of New Kingdom history there were endless attempts to come to terms with the theological problems that these new political realities raised and Ramesses' Kadesh inscriptions are but one solution to this problem, one stage of the retreat from the absolute faith of the Fourth Dynasty. These cognitive dissonances in society caused great problems of cultural disruption. It is the same problem that is faced, although on a different scale, by many peoples today as they attempt to come to terms with the impact of alien and modern technologies on their traditional cultures.

CHAPTER NINE

THE FEUD OF THE TUTHMOSIDES
AND THE PATH OF TRUE LOVE

The New Kingdom and the empire that it made provided a tremendous challenge to the traditional Egyptian view of the world, and gave the whole era a tension and a dynamism that found vigorous expression in the arts. A 'wind of change' blew through the land. Now, it was the city of Thebes, the capital of Egypt and its empire, that was 'the [primeval] mound where the earth came into being', that was 'the pattern for every city', the yardstick by which others should be judged, for 'all are called *city* after the example of Thebes'. One of its gods, Amun, a mysterious deity of the wind and of fertility, was wedded to the goddess Mut and with their child, Khonsu, this trinity became the royal family of the gods – Amun being the 'King of the Gods'. Amalgamated with Re, the supreme deity of Heliopolis, the northern centre of the sun cult near Memphis, a composite god, Amun-Re, was created to be served by a priesthood whose size and wealth was, and has remained, without parallel in the world. Karnak, Amun-Re's Theban temple and the largest religious edifice ever built, was called 'birth place of all the world'.

This religious realignment was a part of the redefinition of the state establishments – the army, the government, the priesthood, even the office of the king – and these traditional groupings were transformed into powerful and, potentially, opposing spheres of influence. But the king oversaw the growth and development of this new order and, although he was a far cry from the god-monarch of the Old Kingdom, he it was who still held the ultimate reins of power. Evidence of this new interface. between the king and his nobles is seen in the decorative schemes in tombs and temples. In the tomb chapels of the administrators and priests we now find large figures of the king appearing as the first minister of the state – the political overseer of the nation. In the temples too, as we have already seen, the royal reliefs show human aspects of the king: his bravery, his prowess with weapons, chariots and boats. In one instance even the skills of the king in designing temple vases are praised.

The cliff bay of Deir el Bahari in western Thebes. The temple of
Hatshepsut is at its centre

All this points to a new understanding, in which the stress is on the king's *human* attributes rather than on his status as a god, a redefinition of the state that took place, of course, inside the usual ambience of conservatism. Although the process was never a smooth one, by the time the centre of Egyptian government had been moved from Thebes to the Delta, at the fall of the New Kingdom around 1000 B.C., it had sustained the empire for some five hundred years and had created some of the most beautiful and enduring memorials of ancient Egypt.

During the course of this five-hundred-year empire there were just a few rulers whose public image was not that of the usual bellicose and politicized kings whose semi-mythical deeds were recorded on the walls of the Theban temples. Such rare exceptions to the general rule are very interesting. For not only do they show us real alternatives to the normal image of the ancient kings, another choice for the society of the day, but their actions and the subsequent official reactions allow us a view of the state machinery in action while in the process of coming to terms with Egypt's most individual pharaohs.

The most obvious example of one such innovator who, apparently, operated as an individual – for surely no one without the prestige and authority of pharaoh himself could have so radically changed Egyptian culture in such a short period of time – was Akhenaten, the king who

The temple of Amun-Re at Karnak

attempted a religious and, therefore, social revolution which would have placed the royal office once again in the particularly individual relationship with the gods that the monarchs of the Old Kingdom enjoyed. It was a genuinely radical attempt to return to some of the roots of the ancient culture, while at the same time accommodating the realities of contemporary society, and it found expression in a bright new art and by the foundation of a new capital city with temples for a single supreme god. It was an ancient Egyptian cultural revolution, an enormous upheaval that was partly an attempt to grasp the national heritage which was felt to be slipping away in a new, international world. It was, however, a cause that was not taken up by Akhenaten's successors, who returned to the more gradual processes of cultural readjustment which had been favoured by their predecessors. Which of the two policies – the radical king's or his conservative successors' – may be judged as the ostriches of an era of international change will remain a matter of political opinion!

Earlier even than Akhenaten's violent attempt to change the direction of the state there had been another, quieter manipulation of the national culture that had also attempted to create a new direction for the empire – this during the reign of a queen, Hatshepsut. But although both these options for the future of the state were first attacked and then ignored in later reigns, these two rulers have left us some of ancient Egypt's finest monuments.

Queen Hatshepsut, a woman who, uniquely, became *king* of Egypt, was the daughter of a soldier, Tuthmosis I, who died after a long reign in about 1512 B.C. Tuthmosis I was succeeded by his son, called, with startling originality Tuthmosis II who, his mummy indicates, was aged about thirty when he died. Hatshepsut, his half-sister, was married to this young king and had borne him at least one child, a girl called Neferure.

Her monuments show us that even as a king's wife, Hatshepsut was not a usual queen. In a remote desert valley behind western Thebes she had a tomb built in the sheer wall of a cliff, almost 180 feet from the ground. In its plan this extraordinary monument was a most scholarly mixture of earlier tombs, its elements derived partly from Middle Kingdom examples and partly from the tomb of Queen Ahmes Nefertiri, a royal ancestor. In common with two other queens of her day, Ahmes Nefertiri had wielded great power in Egypt, and her divine role as the consort of the god was identified by the title of 'the wife of the god Amun'. These three queens had considerable power during the wars of re-unification – one account tells of one queen rallying faint-hearted Theban soldiers and sending them back into battle at a decisive moment of a campaign. All three had great mortuary cults, both at Abydos and Thebes, where their deeds and praises were recorded in texts written in the names of the kings who were their husbands and their sons.

When Tuthmosis II died, his legitimate successor was his only son – a

boy aged about twelve called, again with startling originality, Tuthmosis –
born of a minor princess named Isis. It was normal, therefore, that his
step-mother/aunt Hatshepsut should govern the country and this she did
quite properly for a few years. But then, in an unprecedented step, she
took the throne in co-regency with her young nephew – the only woman to
do so in the course of Egyptian history. This was not accomplished by her
being named as ruling queen on her monuments but as a fully-titled king
and in this she was supported by some of the highest powers in the land.

In a description of her nomination to the kingship, a text inscribed on
the most splendid sanctuary that she built for Amun-Re at Karnak
describes how Amun himself had approved her radical action. For when
his great statue was taken out of the temple in procession it had proceeded on its way without making a 'divine manifestation' towards the

young king Tuthmosis III. In all probability such manifestations consisted of the statue of the god nodding in the direction of the favoured person. Such oracular gestures are usually interpreted as merely institutional mendacities: the political expression of the temple priests who carried the figure of the god, which stood inside a great model boat that was supported on long carrying poles in much the same way as many religious processional objects are today. Despite this rationalization, it is still true that at Thebes today many people who have carried corpses to burial in the local cemeteries find that, on occasion, their loads will dictate by insurmountable pressures, the direction and speed that the corpse wishes to travel. To disbelieve either these modern pall bearers, or the possibility of an ancient statue nodding in assent, simply strips away what is believed to be true and replaces it with the dead-end of modern cynicism.

The statue of Amun, housed in a kiosk on the deck of a sacred bark, is taken on poles carried by the temple priests to visit the god of the Temple of Luxor ; the co-regent Hatshepsut, and Tuthmosis III follow its progress. A quartzite relief from the anciently dismantled sanctuary of Hatshepsut at Karnak

147

Hatshepsut not only secured the approval of the state god but also of his high priest Hapuseneb, a man of long-standing family connections with the throne who remained her loyal supporter throughout the greater part of her reign. The most favoured and most vigorous member of Hatshepsut's court was, however, an official who, though possessed of a vast collection of offices, held no one position of power in the state other than that of being in royal favour throughout virtually the queen's entire reign. The Chief Steward Senmut seems to have been a man of great personality; portraits of him are unusually easy to recognize: a man with a wrinkled small-featured face. His name is so closely linked to Hatshepsut's that it has been claimed that he was her long-standing lover; certainly he was unusually close to his ruler and was also tutor to Princess Neferure until her premature death. While the High Priest Hapuseneb supervised the excavation of a tomb for Hatshepsut in the Valley of the Kings, a monument shaped like one of the Abydos tombs of her Middle Kingdom predecessors, Senmut built great monuments for her at Karnak.

Without embarking upon any lavishly recorded wars of conquest, Hatshepsut lived out her co-regency with Tuthmosis III in much the same way as kings of a thousand years before had: building temples for herself and her family, and monuments for the gods of Egypt. In her mortuary temple, which also contained chapels for the cults of her co-regent and her dead father Tuthmosis I, a long sequence of reliefs showed Hatshepsut's divine origins, the god Amun making love to the amazed figure of her mother, Queen Ahmose who, as a result of this joyful union, gives birth to Hatshepsut. Another series of reliefs showing an expedition to the land of Punt, a foreign country, probably a part of modern-day Somalia or Ethiopia, where the ancient Egyptians obtained incense, aromatics, and trees that were transplanted to the temple precincts in Egypt. Not only is it significant that these most beautiful records in her temple replace the more usual war reliefs, but it is apparent that her expedition went in friendship to the foreign people of Punt and the recording artist shows his lively curiosity of such exotic places by giving a closely detailed record of the inhabitants and their houses – the oldest pictorial records of African tribal life that have survived.

In the depth of the temple's Hathor chapel are a number of reliefs of Senmut, who was in charge of building the temple, and for a mere private person to appear in such a holy place is an otherwise unknown privilege. Perhaps more extraordinary is the fact that, like Hatshepsut, who was buried in a tomb that burrows some 900 feet down from the Valley of the Kings towards her mortuary temple, Senmut too had a tomb quarried deep under the royal temple. And his sarcophagus, like hers, was of quartzite, of virtually royal design, and a unique object to be made by the royal workshops for a private person.

Hatshepsut's mortuary temple, at Deir el Bahari in western Thebes,

Hatshepsut's temple at Deir el Bahari

whose construction Senmut supervised, is one of the greatest works of ancient Egyptian architecture. Whereas most Egyptian temples stand on the landscape, this temple is built into it. It is a unique example of architecture that co-exists with a powerful landscape – in this case a huge semicircular bay of cliffs – without either dominating it or being subordinated by it. The two architectures, man's and nature's, are in a remarkable equilibrium that displays a quite extraordinary ancient sensitivity to environment. Deir el Bahari is one of those places on our planet where a link has been made between earth and heaven. Though ruined, the temple's platforms are still the stages for the gods, the original purposes of the place are still contained within its walls. It stands in a deep hot silence filled with ancient time.

149

Tuthmosis III, in the time-honoured pose, slaughters the enemies of Egypt – in this instance Asiatic captives ; a relief cut on the seventh pylon of the Karnak temple

Like all the other Theban mortuary temples, Hatshepsut's consisted of a series of courtyards, each smaller than the last, each colonnaded and decorated with reliefs cut on the shadowed walls behind rows of columns. And, as in other temples, the floor rises until the central cult chamber is reached. But unlike other temples, this one is not enclosed and each successive courtyard is built at the full height of the façade of the previous courtyard. Thus you walk along high white ramps up through the open temple towards the encircling cliffs where, at their cool centre, the small barrel-vaulted cult chapel of Hatshepsut is cut. And as it rises so dramatically in its landscape, the carefully measured temple may be seen for miles, the only one, in fact, of the Theban mortuary temples of which this is true. To underline this radical difference, this opening-up of the ancient architecture, it should be remembered that all the other large temples of Egypt were originally surrounded by high thick walls of dark grey mud brick and were never visible from outside the sacred enclosure.

Such beautiful and innovative architecture was not achieved without a great deal of thought and this is reflected in the numerous changes in the building's plan. Originally, the temple was to be built in a manner that partly imitated a monument of a Middle Kingdom king that stands, badly ruined, beside it. Hatshepsut's architects re-used the mathematical module of this earlier temple, in a greatly expanded version, in their own building, thus making a visual harmony between the two monuments. A fraction of the same module of 94.5 cubits (49.46 m) was also used for the burial chamber of Hatshepsut's tomb in the Valley of the Kings.

As the Middle Kingdom temple had used all the available area at the foot of the cliffs in the rock bay Hatshepsut's designers were compelled to quarry away the natural slope at the base of the high cliffs to make sufficient room for their new temple. In this way the building was placed into the natural cliff landscape with all the care of a jeweller setting a finely cut stone.

There are many historical precedents for the plan of Hatshepsut's temple but none of these are royal and all are smallish monuments. Hatshepsut's designers took these simple provincial forms, added some of the powerful heraldic elements of decoration that were used on the pyramid temples of the Middle Kingdom, and made a new form of royal architecture. As a temple site, as an especially holy place, this marvellous location was revered for more than a thousand years. But as a symbol of Hatshepsut's earthly success the great temple was subjected to a dire process of ritual 'cleansing' to rid it of the presence of this woman who had dared to be a king.

After waiting for some twenty years to gain exclusive possession of the throne, Tuthmosis III eventually succeeded as sole ruler, presumably at Hatshepsut's death in 1482 B.C. Like other kings of the empire he set out on a series of offensive wars and for years he campaigned in Nubia and throughout the Middle East. Like the records of other warrior kings, his Karnak texts tell of foreign subjects in a state of rebellion and of the land of Egypt ruined, the temples in need of repair. For every king claimed to inaugurate these processes of renewal to bring stability and order to a nation that had just undergone the ritual trauma of the sovereign's death. But it was Tuthmosis III who seems to have established the idea of Imperial Egypt in its mature form.

At a point about midway in his independent reign, Tuthmosis III turned his stone masons onto the monuments of Hatshepsut and the figures of the queen/king were cut from her wall decorations and the beautiful free-standing sculptures that had been an integral part of the architecture of her mortuary temple were all destroyed. Her names were cut from the wall scenes and replaced either by those of Tuthmosis III or his long-dead grandfather, Tuthmosis I – a simple change that was considered sufficient to alter the identity of the figure of Hatshepsut to that of another king. At this time, a stela was set up in the temple at Karnak which told that the statue of Amun-Re *had* indicated that the young Tuthmosis III was intended for the throne of Egypt by the gods! At the same time Hatshepsut's marvellous quartzite shrine, which housed the statue of Amun-Re at Karnak, was dismantled block by block and another set up in its place. Fortunately, the glistening red stones of this building were inadvertently preserved in perfect condition when they were used for filling in another massive building project at Karnak. On

these blocks of quartzite – the hardest of all the ancient building stones – the erasure of Tuthmosis III's masons may also be seen, carefully obliterating the figures and titles of Hatshepsut.

Henceforth, Hatshepsut was officially described as a usurper and her names do not appear in any of the official lists of kings. Like many ancient Egyptians who fell from official grace, she became a non-person. The final phase of the assumption of power by the great queens of the dynasty, which had led to Hatshepsut taking the throne itself, had failed. Egypt was now firmly set on a public course of militarism, and of the enrichment of the national gods with large amounts of foreign war-booty. Endlessly repetitive texts of battles cast in the same mould as the annals of Tuthmosis III, long lists of defeated tribes and nations, and vigorous battle scenes showing fighting kings flooded over the walls of the temples of Egypt. Thus the image of the country as a military empire was firmly established by Tuthmosis III and Egypt finally relinquished the timeless inward-looking attitudes of earlier ages.

Although the figures of Hatshepsut had been carefully hacked from the walls of her mortuary temple at Deir el Bahari, the other figures in the scenes, such as the attendant gods, were not attacked. In many instances the mutilation was made precisely along the outlines of Hatshepsut's

The careful erasure of a figure of Hatshepsut by agents of Tuthmosis III is evidenced by the blurred area at the centre of this relief – another from the queen/king's dismantled sanctuary at Karnak Temple

figures without any effort being made to disguise the fact that her figure had originally been carved on the wall. The figures, then, have been publicly erased but they still exist as negative scratched-out images, and so we may still read the queen's mutilated texts and see her chiselled-out figure on the temple walls. The erasures are, therefore, of a magical nature: the physical removal of an image that held the presence of a person and *not* an attempt to erase Hatshepsut's political presence or to change history.

In common with all such reliefs in Egypt, it is very likely that when these scenes were first finished, ceremonies were performed on them that vitalized their images and put the very spirit of the king into his picture on the wall. Similar magical properties were also held to apply to the texts and their individual hieroglyphs. So, the significance of these graven images was of a very different order to that which today prompts the erasure of a royal cypher, the destruction of an official portrait of a politician.

There are many types of erasures to be seen on royal reliefs, in tomb chapels, and on statues, made at different times in Egyptian history for many motives. Limited mutilation might include just damaging a figure's eye – though some of these are the results of more modern superstition – or cutting through the drawing of an animal or a person. As well as the erasure of the names and figure of Hatshepsut at her Deir el Bahari temple there has also been, in common with the rest of the temples at Thebes, a later erasure of the names and figures of the god Amun-Re by the agents of King Akhenaten – this being one aspect of his attempt to replace the great gods of Thebes with a single national deity of his own choice. Some of these heretical erasures were later restored on the orders of Ramesses II, whose somewhat ham-fisted masons slapped plaster over the mutilated scenes in which they modelled fresh figures and texts. Bald inscriptions that record these restorations were then added to the temple walls. So this splendid temple, though still clean and elegant, has been at different times a battleground of magical, religious, and historical ideas, and the traces of these events – the mutilations, the restorations, and changes in the wall decorations – have been primary sources of information about the events they witnessed.

As the scholars tried to decipher whose names had been erased, whose had been recut, and when these alterations had occurred, the temple walls proved to be as much a battleground for them as it was for the ancient masons. Sometimes the surviving evidence for the changes consists only of the most minute traces of plaster and paint, or of hints of carved hieroglyphs among the rough chisel marks of the erasing masons. And sometimes such clues are so minute that they may only be seen with light directed at the wall from a particular angle. Acute scholarship that can see the historical possibilities in these small marks, and good eyes to see the traces of the ancient chisels, are needed and for many egyptologists this

A part of a large relief in the temple of Hatshepsut at Deir el Bahari shows a plaster restoration of the god Shu (left); one of an assembly of gods erased during the religious reformations of King Akhenaten. The Cromwellian zeal of the agents of these reforms did not, however, extend to the figure of the creator god Atum (right) which is the original figure carved by Hatshepsut's sculptors. An inscription close to this scene says that these erasures were restored by order of Ramesses II who 'renewed these buildings for his father Amun'

155

aspect of their work is the very stuff of history. Whole reigns, indeed, have risen and fallen on the interpretation of such signs.

At the conclusion of a near forty-year debate on the erasures and restorations in Hatshepsut's temple – the 'Feud of the Tuthmosides' as James Breasted dubbed it – a consensus on the broad sequence of events was eventually reached. At first it had been proposed that there was a dramatic encounter between the supporters of Hatshepsut and Tuthmosis III who had whittled away her supporters until finally he was able to have the queen/king done to death and her body destroyed. But then fresh evidence suggested that such a dramatic picture should be modified: that the erasure of the figures and titles of Hatshepsut from her monuments took place later in the reign of Tuthmosis III than had previously been thought: that the king had not acted out of anger or spite but for ritualistic or official reasons. Supporting this re-interpretation, recent excavations in the Valley of the Kings found a long and most elegantly carved piece of wood that came, apparently, from Hatshepsut's coffin. Found in association with similar material from the burial of Tuthmosis III this suggests that he did, in fact, bury his aunt, as he himself was later buried, in the Valley of the Kings.

With a female at the centre of such a singular story it is not surprising that many of the interpretations of these ancient events depend on contemporary attitudes to the role of women in society and, even, the

The unfinished Middle Kingdom tomb above Deir el Bahari whose walls bear the Eighteenth Dynasty graffiti

effects of 'femininity' on architecture and Egyptian militarism have been discussed. Some have portrayed the queen/king as a shrew-like harridan who, with a gang of cronies, inhibited the ambitions of the handsome Tuthmosis III – 'a short stocky man full of Napoleonic energy' – until, in long pent-up frustration, he burst across Asia with his army to create the greatest empire Egypt ever held. Hatshepsut has been variously touted as a pacifist, a protofeminist and a trans-sexual (as king she is pictured in her reliefs as a man). Senmut is judged variously as her lover and the genius who designed and built a beautiful temple for his queen or as a jumped-up opportunist who preyed on a lonely woman! With such slender evidence of history and motives it is as well to keep one's personal experience of 'human nature' (i.e. of modern Western man) well away from the affair of Hatshepsut and her times, for here we deal with ancient and mysterious motivations. There is nothing in the remains of the monuments of Hatshepsut, Senmut or Tuthmosis III that can tell us what the three protagonists *thought* about their situation. We are left only with the residue of *official* actions which, as we are only too well aware, provide a strangely distorted reflection. Quite remarkably, however, there are some rare contemporary documents which may hint at what Hatshepsut's contemporaries thought about these events.

High above the top terrace of Hatshepsut's temple at the height of a row of Middle Kingdom nobles' tombs that decorate the huge rock bay, is a small unfinished tomb of the same period. It is a cave-like hole cut into the limestone cliff that, apart from a carefully scribbled Middle Kingdom text on one of its walls, remained empty and unused for some five hundred years until it was taken over by some of the officials while they were employed apparently on the construction of Hatshepsut's temple below. Here, these officials stored their water and beer and here, in all probability, they retired to sit in the quiet shade offered by the tomb. The encircling cliffs not only focused the sun's rays onto the temple far below them but also sheltered it from any relieving breeze – for a brief while at the end of the last century, Deir el Bahari held the world's temperature record!

On the walls of the sheltering cave, Hatshepsut's supervisors and scribes wrote their names and titles in inks, colours and engravings. Some are laid-out by men whose obvious skill with a brush makes it apparent that writing was their usual trade, while others were evidently less used to the delicate art of writing hieroglyphics. In fact, some of these inscriptions and drawings are so rough that it is difficult to believe that the writers had not drunk rather too much of the beer whose empty jars still lie in heaps on the floor. This ancient beer, which was far removed from our modern hop-flavoured beverage, was made in dozens of different ways. Brewing was a varied art like that of the confectioner. One surprising method was to soak bread and a little dough in water until the natural fermentation produced a thick porridge-like mess that was sufficiently strong to attract the moralizing writings of temperate-minded scribes who warned of its evil effect and the lives that had been ruined by drinking to excess.

Our ancient cave-dwellers, however, do not seem to have heeded the abolitionists and their eyrie supplied them with an ideal pavilion for viewing the work in the temple below while at the same time it also gave them a fine view right across the cultivated plain to the river, allowing them ample warning of the arrival of the great officials such as Hapuseneb or Senmut at the temple. And Senmut, apparently, was much in the minds of these officials, for on one wall of their cave there is a particularly wretched drawing of him. There is another, made in a precise manner by a good hand, in which the Overseer of the House of Amun also seems to figure. This graffito shows two people engaged in sexual intercourse, the woman standing and bending over, the man at her back. But for a strange-shaped hat, the man is naked. Now this hat is not common in ancient Egyptian art but it does sometimes make an appearance on the heads of supervisors, where it was probably made of leather. Most helpfully, another figure drawn by this same hand just a few feet along the wall from this amorous couple is wearing a similar hat, and this figure stands in the traditional attitude of the supervisor. The supervisor at Deir el Bahari was, of course, Senmut, the 'Lord High Everything Else' of Hatshepsut's reign, as he has been aptly dubbed.

The nude figure who is so engaging the supervisor's attentions in this small graffito is a most curious drawing. Despite the male proportions of her body and her lack of breasts it is certainly intended to represent a woman. Three other nude males appear on the same wall and all have ludicrously enlarged genitalia, a feature that this figure quite lacks. Furthermore, in the muddled drawing of a midriff a black triangle may be seen. This is a most Egyptian sign of gender that was drawn on all paintings of female nudes and was carefully modelled on most sculptured female torsos. This woman also wears a royal wig. Now, from all the periods of ancient Egyptian history there is but one person who would fit this curious iconography, and that is Hatshepsut, Senmut's queen. Here, perhaps, we should not expect the appearance of the ureus – the ever-present royal emblem of a cobra worn on the king's forehead – for the artist is making a precise comment on the ambiguity of the queen/king's role, being disrespectful not to the sacred king but to a mere usurping woman. That the artist really was intending to be disrespectful is borne out by the style of his work. Of all the pornography that has survived from ancient Egypt this drawing alone is not made in the hasty manner of most ribald scenes or as a scurrilous satire on religious representations. This drawing is careful and deliberate with some noticeable hesitations at exactly those points in the figure which distinguish it as a woman and a king. It is, apparently, an acid comment on Hatshepsut and her court by a contemporary observer that, uniquely, shows the rulers as people; and it seems that neither Hatshepsut nor Senmut measured up to this artist's ideas of a dignified government. And that they did not is underlined by the artist's use of pornography in this context: for the ancient Egyptians were almost as reticent about their sexual life as modern historians have been about dealing with the ancient evidence.

This is a pity for, with all our differences, we still share with our most ancient predecessors the basic traits of humanity. They too walked on earth, engendered and protected their own kind and then died. If then, the

One of the walls of the tomb above Deir el Bahari that Hatshepsut's managers used as a blackboard for their graffiti; many names have been drawn and carved on it. The figure of the supervisor is slightly right of centre; the pornographic graffiti is underneath the carefully written text, which is drawn between ruled lines

ancient Egyptians represented sexual intercourse only a few dozen times in the course of their long history we might assume that it was a subject which, unlike in our own times, was regarded with universal reticence. However, accurate statistics are hard to come by, for much of this 'questionable' art is presently locked up in museum storerooms!

The ancient Egyptians, however, were not by modern standards prudish. Many people wore virtually no clothes during the hot Egyptian summers and some of the finest ladies in the land wore gowns that were transparent or that left their breasts uncovered. On the temple walls some gods appear with penis erect and stoutly grasped in one hand. Dancing girls wore nothing but elaborate tattoos and strings of waistline beads. They also had a richly imaged love poetry of great beauty. Romantic love,

An alabaster figurine of the Middle Kingdom (The Louvre)

at least during the New Kingdom, seems to have been a recognized social force. These poems almost bring to us the breath of young couples as they experience sentiments which appear more straight forward and more modern than those expressed in much European literature of the past few hundred years.

> She looks like the rising morning star
> At the start of a happy year.
> Shining bright, fair of skin,
> Lovely the look of her eyes,
> Sweet the speech of her lips,
> She has not a word too much.
> Upright neck, shining breast,
> Hair true lapis lazuli;
> Arms surpassing gold,
> Fingers like lotus buds.
> Heavy thighs, narrow waist,
> Her legs parade her beauty;
> With graceful step she treads the ground,
> Captures my heart by her movements.

Another collection of these texts begins with these words: 'Beginning of the sweet sayings found in a text collection, made by the scribe of the necropolis, Nakht-Sobk.'

> How well she knows to cast the noose,
> And yet not pay the cattle tax!
> She casts the noose on me with her hair,
> She captures me with her eye;
> She curbs me with her necklace,
> She brands me with her seal ring.
> Why do you argue with your heart?
> Go after her, embrace her!

And from a collection of songs on a papyrus entitled 'Beginning of the delightful, beautiful songs of your beloved sister as she comes from the fields.'

> My heart thought of my love of you,
> When half of my hair was braided;
> I came at a run to find you,
> And neglected my hairdo.
> Now if you let me braid my hair,
> I shall be ready in a moment.

Other poems also tell of lovers' trysts and traps – but all with exultation and without the inherent afflictions of much modern love poetry. The poems also describe the ancient world inhabited by the lovers – not the lavish parties of their elders that were so often painted by the ancient tomb artists – but of gangs of young people enjoying themselves, of lush green gardens with pools of cool water (in which a girl might immerse herself in her finest robe so as to appear naked to her lover), of bouts of drinking under trees on long hot afternoons, of flowers, of the sensual fineness of precious stones and metals, fruit and, perhaps more than anything, of perfumes.

It is striking that in their love poetry the Egyptians used many of the same metaphors that were used in religious contexts. Gods too were offered aphrodisiacs (in the form of flowering lettuces) and were surrounded with the same precious materials with which adoring lovers were so fond of comparing each other. In the state religion too we may find the same splendid hedonism of the love poetry rather than the tenets for personal behaviour or morality. The gods themselves ran the entire range of sexual behaviour from the raping of the young Horus by his uncle Seth to the revitalizing of the corpse of Osiris by his wife who, transformed into a bird, hovers over her husband, gently fanning his body with her wings.

At Deir el Bahari, in the account of Hatshepsut's divine origins, there is a powerful description of the visitation of Amun-Re to her mother. The King of the Gods had entered the form of King Tuthmosis I for the occasion:

> This august god found her as she slept in the beauty of her palace. She awoke because of the savour of the god and she laughed in the presence of his majesty. He came to her straight away. He was ardent for her. He gave his heart unto her. He let her see him in the form of a god after he came before her. She rejoiced on beholding his beauty: his love went through her body. The palace was filled with the savour of the god, and his odours were as those of Punt. Then the majesty of this god did all that he desired with her. She let him rejoice over her, she kissed him.

The queen was suitably impressed with her night visitor:

> How great is your fame! It is splendid to see your front: you have united me with your favours, your dew is in all my limbs.

It is to be hoped that such fine texts will serve to rescue the ancient Egyptians from the monastic desert-like limbo into which they are usually cast. By modern standards they were, perhaps, more reticent than us. But the delight in life that they continually show us in their art and architecture, the fine sensuality of their painting and sculpture, their concern with life in both people and animals, is reflected briefly but strongly in the surviving fragments of their literature of romance and love.

*Amun visits Queen Ahmose in her palace ; the god is touching her
nose – a seat of joy and life – with the* ankh, *a heiroglyphic sign that
signifies 'life'. A drawing by Howard Carter of a relief in the temple
of Hatshepsut at Deir el Bahari*

163

CHAPTER TEN

SONS AND LOVERS

For the inhabitants of ancient Thebes, the plain that lay opposite their town, on the west bank of the wide river, was a friendly place filled with the benevolent spirits of ancestors and dead kings that had become a part of the sun's power, the miracle of the annual flood and of the sprouting seed. These primal powers of potency and fertility were not only accessible in the vast cemeteries and great temples, but were also mysteriously omnipresent in the adjacent Valley of the Kings where, deep down in the royal tombs, the mystical processes that surrounded the cycles of royal death, procreation and resurrection interwove.

Modern critics – fundamentalists – have called the New Kingdom an age of ever increasing religious decadence, of doubt, fear, and superstition: the slow decaying of the ancient faith. In fact it was an age of new directions in theology as the Theban priests recast the ancient religion to conform to the dynamics of a new era of history. New texts systematized the old writings that had described the destinies of the royal dead; new method was introduced into the old religion; for example, constellations that marked, by their rising and falling the stages of the royal resurrection were identified early in the New Kingdom and later these made their appearance in the Theban royal tombs as great ceilings of star charts. And objects that dealt precisely with some of these newly defined aspects of the royal destiny were laid in the tombs, which became great depositaries of ritual equipment and information for the dead monarch.

Western Thebes was now the domain of a great mother goddess: Hathor 'the Golden One' – the Golden Calf of the Old Testament. Several different forms of this goddess, usually those of a beautiful woman or a huge brown cow, were common in the monuments of the Theban cemeteries. Hathor was one of the most ancient of all the Egyptian gods whose symbols can be traced back to predynastic times. An aspect of the Great Goddess, Hathor

The mountain peak called 'The Gurn' looming over the Valley of the Kings. The two doorways in the foreground of the picture are the entrances of two royal tombs; Seti I's, left, and Ramesses I's, right

was at once a lover, a mother, a bawd and also a ferocious avenging lion, a goddess of music, of gold, of drunkenness and of dancing. She was also identified as the starry sky whose celestial milk had suckled the infant kings of Egypt. Hatshepsut identified herself with Hathor on the sculptured capitals of the goddess that stood in the Hathor chapel of her mortuary temple, for they have the fine features of the queen/king's faces on them.

Hathor was the mother of Horus, the king of Egypt; her name, Hat-Hor literally means 'the house of Horus'. Necessarily, Horus was also identified as the child of Osiris and Isis for, as King of the Underworld at one with the dead king, Osiris's paternity of the ruler of Egypt ensured his legitimacy.

The king drinking from the udder of the Hathor cow. A relief on a
wall of the temple of Ramesses II at Abydos

As the son of Isis, Horus rejoiced in the attentions of the goddess who epitomized the virtues of mother love and devotion. As the son of Hathor, Horus inherited this goddesses's cosmological attributes: all the movements of the universe, those of the sun, the sky, the moon, the stars and, even, the wind. So, as son of Hathor, Horus finds his potential in his role as a cosmic lord fulfilling his destiny of eternal resurrection. 'Take my breast that you may drink, so that you may live again', says Hathor to her son in one of the pyramid texts; it is the milk of heaven that she offers the king of Egypt; this goddess is concerned with the nourishment and with the dynamics of the king's eternal resurrection.

The golden cliffs of Western Thebes were regarded as the domain of, even as the very body of, Hathor and the tombs excavated in them were the goddess's womb. Drawings in many of the tombs' chapels show the Hathor

Above *The Hathor cow that, for some three and a half thousand years suckled a sculptured Tuthmosis III in the darkness of her closed sanctuary, stands freshly revealed in the sunlight – 2 pm, 12 February 1906. The sanctuary and the sacred cow are now in the Cairo Museum*

Right *Tuthmosis III suckled by the Isis tree. A drawing on the face of a column in the burial chamber of the king's tomb*

cow standing patiently above the western mountains waiting for the return of her children who were living on the east bank of the river. At the turn of the last century, archeologists working at Deir el Bahari were surprised to find this mythic image turned to reality when they uncovered a huge sculpture of a Hathor cow standing in a small chapel cut into the cliff above Hatshepsut's temple. Her horns hold the sun and are surrounded by the papyrus plants of the Delta that was her traditional homeland. A figure of the child-king Tuthmosis III kneels to take the milk from her udder; the goddess suckles the child as she will later succour the man entombed in the depths of her golden mountain.

In his choice of burial site Tuthmosis III followed Hatshepsut to the Valley of the Kings which he established as the royal burial ground of the New Kingdom. His tomb is the first example of the style typical of all the later royal tombs; it is the fountainhead of their designs.

Many elements in the design of his tomb were taken from the two earlier tombs that had been made for Hatshepsut, but here they were all brought together and welded into one design. Similarly, Tuthmosis III's sarcophagus also followed the pattern established by his aunt, who had commissioned three such superb quartzite boxes for her father and herself.

As the tomb was identified as a womb so, especially, was the royal coffin. A thousand years after Hatshepsut's time, a Greek visitor to Egypt recorded a folk story about a king's daughter who was buried in a cow-shaped coffin and a legend that described how the dead king Osiris was placed into a wooden cow by Isis and covered with fine linens. The two goddesses, Hathor and Isis, shared many of the same qualities and their identities were interlaced around the figure of the dead king. In a beautiful drawing on one of the two columns in the burial chamber of the tomb of Tuthmosis III it is not Hathor who offers her breast to the king, but the goddess Isis – whose name had also been taken by the king's physical mother, one of his father's concubines.

Here, however, Isis is not shaped as a slender young woman who, with her sister Nepthys, decorated so many of the royal sarcophagi, but as a tree, and her breast hangs from one of its branches. In a splendid transposition of images, it is this same tree, a sycamore fig, from which the royal coffins are made – the goddess's womb to which the king returns during the processes of his resurrection.

When the king died, his body was subjected to the rituals that encompassed these same dramas of resurrection, rituals that, in slightly

A splendid relief showing the king undergoing ritual washing. The water has been replaced by hieroglyphs signifying 'life' and 'stability', which flow in graceful arcs from two temple vessels held over the king's head. A limestone block from a dismantled temple of Amenhotep I at Karnak

The burial chamber of Tuthmosis III in the Valley of the Kings

different forms, had taken place in the temples at the daily attendance upon the statues of the gods for thousands of years. As the living king was regarded as a sun god who was bathed in the waters of Nun before appearing upon the eastern horizon, so the king was washed in a daily ritual in which he was attended by two priests dressed as gods. The dead king, too, underwent the same ritual washing during the process of mummification. This washing took place after the body had been taken from the bed of natron that had absorbed most of its fat. The water used to wash the royal corpse had been taken from the Nile at Aswan, a part of the river's rising flood, and was identified as the fertile water that had issued from the body of the dead Osiris, with whom the king would be identified after his introduction into the Underworld. The rituals performed on the dead kings with this water employed the same splendid vessels as those used in the daily rites performed on the living king. Many fine examples of this ritual equipment have been found in the Valley of the Kings, those from Tutankhamen's tomb being particularly well preserved and well known. Along with their personal possessions and the shrine-encased statues of the gods – so that the dead kings would, literally, be in their presence – these ritual objects formed the glittering-rich contents of the royal tombs in the Valley of the Kings.

It is likely that the ceremonies, connected with the resurrection of the dead king, were performed in concert with movements of the heavens. The dead king was washed at sunrise to be taken to the Valley of the Kings and down into the corridors of his tomb and laid in the sarcophagus that stood in the burial chamber. In the earliest tombs in the Valley this chamber was without sunlight: the total darkness of the underworld.

Texts on the burial chamber walls tell us what happens in this great darkness. As the god Re opens the doors of the Underworld for the king and makes ready for his ritual descent into the infernal regions, so this strange demi-world breathes again with the power that is come into it; the darkness is lit by the dead king. And, as if to paraphrase the entire results of this long drama, the beginnings of which are stirring, larva-like, in the darkness of the tomb, the dead king now enters an enormous serpent and, as he moves through this long dark tunnel, he abandons his flesh and is reborn, as a new sun at its rising, in the shape of a scarab beetle that emerges from the serpent's mouth.

The text that describes the journeys and combats of the king as he passes through the twelve hours of the night through the Underworld on his way to his daily resurrection was called *Amduat* (The Book of that which is in the Otherworld) and it was written in many royal tombs including that of Tuthmosis III. It describes not only the royal resurrection but also the elemental forces of the agrarian calendar with which the power of the royal resurrection was identified. Although the status of the king may have become somewhat secularized during the New Kingdom, nevertheless, in death he regained the significance of the godly life-giver of the land of Egypt, the age-old function of Pharaoh.

Amduat is a triumph of New Kingdom theology, a vital part of the coming to terms with the changing world that had its political expression in the new image of empire and its religious expression in the partial codification of the old beliefs of Egyptian religion. Previously these had never been recorded as coherent entities and were shown only in dislocated fragments. However, the religious 'books' of New Kingdom theology, of which *Amduat* is but one example, were a codification and unification of these age-old beliefs, made by the priests pressurized by the acute inquiries of a new era. *Amduat* tells of the life, rebirth and death of the creative energies of the universe embodied in the god Re, who is identified with the dead king. The *Amduat* that was drawn on the walls of Tuthmosis III's burial chamber is like the writings on a huge papyrus roll and is, in fact, a giant version of a smaller original text, made with great speed and skill by four scribes at a time shortly after the king had been laid in his sarcophagus.

Amduat divides the processes of the royal resurrection into twelve night hours, each one of which is a separate incident in the journey to rebirth. The hours are named as goddesses, and some of the universal terrors of death and the hopes for resurrection are held in their names: 'She who cleaves the brow of the enemies of Re', 'She who cuts up souls' and the Twelfth, triumphant ultimate hour, is called 'She who sees the beauty of her Lord'.

The texts start with a clear description of their awesome contents:

> The writings of the hidden chamber. The places where the souls, the gods and the spirits stand. What they do. The beginning of the Horn of the West, the gate of the Western Horizon. This is the knowledge of what they do: the knowledge of their sacred rituals to Re; knowledge of the mysterious powers; knowledge of what is in the hours as well as of their gods; knowledge of what he says to them; knowledge of the gates [the entrances to the Underworld] and the ways on which the great god passes; knowledge of the movements of the hours and their gods; knowledge of the powerful ones and the annihilated . . .

During the twelve night hours, Re grants land to the god of grain; Mind and Will to Osiris, the Lord of the Underworld; and all the god's enemies are executed. The progress of the king, a description of the life-sustaining processes of the country, revolves ultimately around the royal resurrection, when he will appear on the eastern horizon, shining at dawn as the sun god. In the Fourth Hour the king reaches the desolate bottom of the Underworld and the boat on which the king makes his nightly journey, a vessel filled with gods and personifications of aspects of the royal personality, is transformed into a two-headed snake that lights the deep darkness with flames that flare from its mouth: 'The flames coming out of the mouths of the barge guide him towards the mysterious ways. He does not see their forms. He calls to them and it is his words they hear.' The dead king, in the last moments before the resurrection moves in a lightless, formless void across the primeval waters. In part, this is an invocation of the beginning of the world, the formless void from which life first emerged.

It is the Fifth Hour that sees the climax for the struggle for the royal rebirth, here:

The image of the king is in darkness. The egg that belongs to it has light in it, the flesh shines, the legs inside are in coils. Noise is heard in the egg after the Great God has passed like the sound of roaring in the sky during a storm.

The images of change, deep and unfathomable, pile one upon the other. This larval king bursts from his egg and sits on the shoulders of the sphinxes of the horizon; and as he bursts forth, so the sun appears at the

The Twelfth, and final, Hour of Amduat: *the beetle pushes the sun through the sand of the horizon* (right) *while underneath, the king's mummy remains in the Underworld*

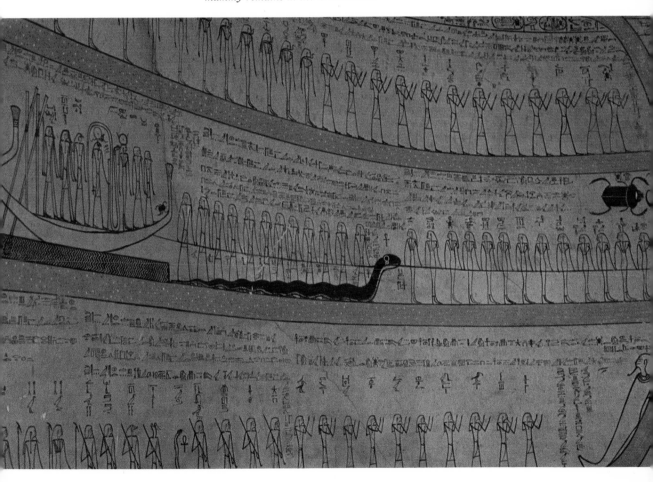

new day's dawning. Other images of the same event, all thrusting up and up through the frame of the picture, are piled above. The little scarab beetle pushes his way through the dark sand towards the horizon, the stomach of a snake that had swallowed the god disgorges him and aided by a great regiment of gods using magical ropes the king is inexorably pulled, pushed and projected towards his predestined rebirth. The magic power of this upward force is exemplified in the way that the artist has bent the register lines that frame these pictures. Very seldom does the basic framework of ancient Egyptian art bend under the force of the images that it contains!

The Twelfth Hour, the celebration of the royal rebirth, an antique Halleluja Chorus, sees the king finally established on the eastern horizon while his mummy remains in the Underworld worshipped by an immense gathering of gods. It is a triumphal scene. Now, the Egyptians were not as stupid to imagine that without these attentions the sun would not rise in the morning; but these precise images of this mysterious process gave their faith shape; an ordered belief without which, they perceived, man would float in formless terror, with no meaning to either life or death.

In *Amduat* the ancient scribes are grasping at careful descriptions of death becoming life, and they move instinctively towards this esoteric subject using the signs and symbols of the ancient religion, all painted on the walls of the royal burial chambers with a directness and clarity that comes from strict exactitude of thought. Later, this clear and profound religious statement was amplified and enlarged to include the demon-filled nightmares that described more of the horrors of death than of the mysteries of resurrection but in the tomb of Tuthmosis III we see one of the finest expressions of New Kingdom faith in one of its most beautiful settings.

The great burial chamber in the tomb, where the long text of *Amduat* sweeps right around the oval walls, is neither lavish in its size nor gaudy in its decoration. It has, in fact, that indefinable mix of good taste and excellent craftsmanship that is shared by most of the elegant products of mankind. And in its modest splendours it holds more perfection and more liveliness than many of the larger, more bombastic tombs of the later kings. The burial chamber is planned to within fractions of an inch but it is reached after passing through tunnel-like corridors that twist and turn through the natural rock of the Valley in a deliberate attempt to dislocate both direction and time. This *is* the Underworld, 'the Place where the Gods stand'. The later, but unplundered, tomb of Tutankhamen still held its gods, each one gilded, sealed and boxed in shrines standing close by the royal sarcophagus. But Tuthmosis III's tomb was never filled with such lavish things; here the ritual requirements were stripped to a minimum. The architecture, its decoration and the equipment left in the tomb, made it a single machine-like apparatus for the resurrection in which faith was stripped to its functional necessities.

Although it was perhaps a quite unconscious expression of the condition in which the royal dead were thought to be, it is interesting that all the New Kingdom kings, like those before them who were buried in pyramids, were laid in burial chambers that were literally situated under a mountain of stone. And inside the deep burial chamber, the royal corpse was surrounded by shrine after shrine, inside which was a sarcophagus with a heavy stone lid. And inside the sarcophagus were three elaborate coffins, and inside these lay the royal corpse, fitted as tightly as a glove and bound firmly with bandages. It is an extraordinary expression of agoraphobia felt on behalf of the royal dead, a tense stillness protected by a massive system of physical and ritual protection against the forces of evil encountered by the dead king on the journey to his daily resurrection. The king's mummy was bound, encased and entombed to provide for its eternal destiny; the royal fate of an afterlife of tension and movement; an expression of the dynamic equilibrium that was held in the living world; a balance which has often been perceived by people of many different cultures:

> At the still point of the turning world. Neither flesh nor
> fleshless;
> Neither from nor towards; at the still point, there the dance
> is . . .

The royal sarcophagus, the box of stone that held the encoffined king, is seen at its finest in the tomb of Tuthmosis III. By the side of the royal head, as the king lay in his coffins, is a carving of a false door, its design descended directly from the façades of the palaces of the Archaic Period. Here, it is still used as a 'looking glass' – a medium of communication between the living and the dead. Middle Kingdom mummies in similarly shaped sarcophagi actually faced sideways 'looking out' through the false door. Tuthmosis III, however, was laid facing upwards and it was the royal spirit that passed from the physical remains of the king in his sarcophagus down to his mortuary temple which stood among the line of royal temples below, in the plain of Western Thebes.

The temple is gone now, stripped to its pavements by stone robbers, and in modern times a road has been built right through its principal courtyard. Like the Temple of Hatshepsut, this too had a sun chapel, a shrine for Anubis and Hathor and, at the focal point of the building, a chapel for the cult of the king. And here, in the chapel of Tuthmosis III, on the rear wall, right at the back of the temple, stood another false door, about ten feet high and made of pink Aswan granite. Like the false doors that stood in the temples at the feet of the pyramids, this was the place where the spirit of the dead king came from his tomb to enjoy the offerings of his mortuary cult and also to oversee the country he had once ruled.

Long since taken from its temple, this false door now stands at Medinet

Habu, where it was set up by archaeologists who found that it had been used by a Macedonian king as a pylon doorsill. In its plainness, in its careful design and its coolness, it is of the highest standards of Egyptian art. Each line of the carefully designed text is measured in relationship to each other. The hieroglyphs have subtle rhythms in them; they have pictorial as well as religious expression. Above the central 'door' in the stone is a square panel that is the root of the overall geometric composition. It shows a simple scene of the god Amun giving life to Tuthmosis III. Small, drawn well and lightly engraved it does not detract from the rhythmic geometry of the whole.

It is easy to forget that these formally laid out hieroglyphs are, in fact, designs of great skill. In works such as Tuthmosis III's great false doorway, the artists have lifted their perennial task far above the usual standards of the hieroglyphic texts that covered the temple walls; they turned their 'typography' into art. This extreme concentration of skill, the care with which each sign is placed in the design, is just what we should expect from such an essential feature of a great king's mortuary temple and, indeed, this is emphasized by the fact that the door was made in granite, not the softer limestone and sandstone of the rest of the temple.

The almost uncanny perfection of designs such as Tuthmosis III's tomb or his false door has an intellectual and practical intensity that, in our age, is reserved for works of technology, electronics, optics and the like. And in a sense, the work of making the door and the hidden tomb has much in common with those disciplines, for it too was involved in communication and in transmitting physical and mental energies. The royal burial chamber and the false door of the mortuary temple were two points from which the power of the dead king was manifested and from which it emanated; they are the very tip of ancient technology and they have the same elegance and utility as a space module or the supersonic Concorde.

The 'false door' from the mortuary temple of Tuthmosis III, now
re-erected at Medinet Habu

CHAPTER ELEVEN

STILL LIFE

Unlike most of the artists and sculptors of ancient Egypt, those who worked in the royal tombs of the Valley of the Kings are known by name and at Thebes, at a site that has been excavated during the past eighty years, you can visit the village where they lived and the tombs in which they were buried. It is one of the very few places in Egypt where you can still experience something of the everyday lives of the ancient people, where you may stand in the spaces where they lived and walk the ancient village paths. And because of a special accomplishment that was unusually widespread in this village – literacy – there is also preserved a detailed record of their lives, scrawled on pieces of pottery and flakes of limestone. Museums throughout the world exhibit these people's personal possessions: their clothes, furniture, food, and craftsmen's tools.

This remarkable community were experts of death and burial. Generation after generation had made the royal tombs and some of the objects that went in them: statues, shrines, the royal coffins and the like. And as the scribes who supervised the craftsmen kept working records, some of which have also survived, we may know who was absent on a particular day, and why; how many copper chisels were issued for quarrying and cutting the reliefs; how many wicks were issued for the oil lamps that lit their work in the dark tombs; how many days there were in the working week; how many feast days they had; even, who did the laundry!

It is a rare chance to see the realities of the ancient world as opposed to the ideal existence shown in the official versions on tomb and temple walls. Today, this ancient village is called Deir el Medineh after a Christian monastery that was later built there. It is situated in a small desert valley in the middle of the nobles' cemeteries and is connected to the Valley of the Kings by a two-mile-long path. For most of its length this track runs along the ridge of cliffs that overlooks the line of royal mortuary temples, the River Nile and the cultivated fields, Karnak and its temples, and all

Inhirkha'a, a foreman of a gang that worked in the royal tombs of the Valley of the Kings, relaxes with his children. From a scene in his tomb at Deir el Medineh in western Thebes

the ancient city of Thebes. It is still one of the greatest walks in the world.

The differences between the people of this village and the other communities of ancient Egypt are emphasized by its strange location miles away from either water or fertile soil. This village of artists and craftsmen was unique in ancient Egypt and its strange desert setting has preserved it.

As a department of government the village was supported by taxes of food and supplies levied on the area of Thebes and drawn, in monthly rations, from the royal mortuary temples down by the fields. The village had no well and the villagers owned no land. Teams of donkeys daily brought water up to the village and their attendants ran errands for the little community and so kept it in touch with the other settlements and towns about Thebes. The village had its own fishermen who supplied large amounts of dried and fresh fish caught in the Nile. Their laundry was done by specially employed washerwomen down by the river. The men worked in the royal tombs in ten-day shifts and so the village was, for most of the time, filled with the elderly, the women and the children of the seventy-odd families that, typically, made up the community. The desert houses baked throughout the summer and nearly froze during January.

These expert tomb-makers made interesting work of their own tombs. The men who made Pharaoh's underworld were free to make their own small monuments exactly as they wanted using the hereditary skills of the professions that they had practised for a lifetime. The omissions and commissions in their tombs' decorations, the skills they cared to display as opposed to those they employed only in the official arts of the royal tombs, all tell us of local tastes and traditions. In their tombs, built just outside the village walls, generations of families were buried in vaults excavated under small painted chapels – an arrangement similar to the tombs of the nobles. At Deir el Medineh the living were separated from the dead by about a hundred yards and, deep in the burial chambers, their ancestors lay in brightly decorated tombs filled with the handiwork of their families and friends.

Nothing remains of the sites where the dead of the Theban area were mummified. It seems likely that this was done in light tents, 'pavilions of life', made of rush matting that was easily erected and then destroyed after each embalment. The process of mummification lasted two or three months and basically consisted of rendering the fat from the body by covering it with natron – this after all the soft tissue, whose putrefaction might destroy the structure of the corpse, was removed by processes of cutting and dissolving. In fact, such an elaborate method was hardly necessary in Upper Egypt: Tutankhamen's corpse, for example, was virtually destroyed by the embalmer's oils sealed inside the golden coffin, whereas the predynastic inhabitants of Nagada have survived almost twice as long after merely being buried in the warm sandy gravel.

After the traditional rituals of the embalming, the múmmy, wrapped in linens, was returned to the family house at Deir el Medineh to be placed in its coffins. In the village there were several coffin makers and other craftsmen who were responsible for decorating and varnishing. The number of receipts and bills that have survived relating to tomb goods, and to coffins in particular, suggest that these expensive items were a source of great preoccupation for the villagers throughout their lives.

On the day of the funeral, a small procession with the mummy and its coffins pulled on a wooden sledge, left the village and made its way up the western hill beside the village. The villagers built great wide staircases to the tombs; these had low steps with a central slide for the funeral sledge and were similar in shape to those that they made for the upper section of some of the kings' tombs. Frequently, the little tomb chapels, made in the

The ancient village at Deir el Medineh seen from the hillside of tombs

*Tombs of the families who lived in the ancient village at
Deir el Medineh*

shape of steep-sided miniature pyramids were decorated with scenes
inside, such as the dead man and his family receiving offerings, gods such
as Hathor and her Western Mountain, or the village's patron deities –
Ahmes Nefertiri and Amenhotep I. The chapels were constructed of
mud bricks and capped with a single stone that was sometimes carved
with prayers and pictures of the tomb's owner.

The last rites of the funeral took place in front of the tomb chapel while
the coffin, its mummy inside it, stood upright by the door. The most
important of these ceremonies was the 'Opening of the Mouth'. This was
yet another variation of the basic ritual of vivification that was performed
on the reliefs of the temples and the statues of the king when those images
were ritually filled with the spirit of the person that they represented. At
the tomb, of course, it was the mummy that was revitalized, filled again
with the being of the dead person, a spirit that had wandered dangerously
since its physical death. How vulnerable were both the spirit and the
corpse before their ritual establishment in the next world at this time
of funeral!

The 'Opening of the Mouth' ritual is a common subject in the decorations of the tomb chapels at Thebes in which many stages of this long

ceremonial are depicted. To inquire into the origins of such rituals is to realize that even in this most elaborate phase of ancient civilization, when the New Kingdom held a social and political life of great intricacy, the faith of the Egyptians was still drawn from the beliefs and sensitivities of

A painting in the tomb of Nakhtamun at Deir er Medineh. The coffins holding his mummy and that of Nubtemsheset, his wife, stand outside their pyramid-shaped chapel before the rituals of the burial service begin. The western mountain behind the tomb, represented as patterns of dotted lines, almost make this an ancient landscape painting. Nakhtamun was a sculptor who worked in the royal tombs and also as a priest at a small shrine by the village

183

pre-history; motivated by the same pre-occupations that had produced the arts of the Nagada cemeteries, and of the pyramids and their temples.

The proceedings began with the mummy and its case being propped up against the chapel wall and faced towards the south. It stood on a heap of clean desert sand – its own primeval mound that was the stage for the rebirth to follow. Ritual formulae were repeated and different gods were invoked to join in the ceremonies. Animals were slaughtered and offered to the mummy – a favourite offering being the leg of a calf, the living blood still frothing from its veins. This ancient rite which, as we may see in the detail of their drawings, some Egyptian artists regarded as barbaric, was occasionally represented with the mutilated calf standing on its remaining legs while the mother cow, its eyes filled with tears, licked its wound. After this episode, the mummy was decorated with a special headress and a fine broad necklace of flowers and small leaves mixed with beads – these being a common ornament of the coffins and painted on them long before the ceremonies took place. Little balls of natron, an essential ingredient of embalming, were then offered to the mummy as an agent of purification – the officials of this ceremonial had themselves been drinking a solution of natron salts for several days before the funeral to achieve a condition of ritual purity. Then the lips of the coffin's face were moistened with cow's milk, its eyes were painted with cosmetics and incense was burnt. A strange-shaped adze, with a special cutting blade of flint was touched on the coffin's mouth. Slowly the spirit of the dead person repossessed the corpse from which, in the future, it might now freely leave and return. Then as the rituals neared completion, the coffins were lifted away from the chapel's side by a group of men who, with another burning incense before them, took it into the burial chamber below.

As the coffins were taken out of the bright sunlight there was a dramatic ritual gesture by the women mourners that betrayed some of the universal human emotions of such moments. The women, reluctant to allow their kin to depart from them, took hold of the coffin and struggled with the bearers in an attempt to keep it from the tomb. An ancient Egyptian song also acknowledges the fear and dismay at death and the unknown:

> Death is incontestable and we know nothing of what lies beyond:
> No one returns from beyond the grave to tell us how they are,
> to tell us what they need or to relieve our hearts
> until we have also gone there,
> wither they have gone.

Inevitably, however, the coffin party wins the struggle against the women mourners. Another of these reflective songs tells the fearful not to belittle

A restored tomb chapel, shaped like a pyramid, with the shaft that leads to its burial chamber lying open before it

185

the land of the dead: 'The right and just that has no terrors', for

> No one may linger in the land of Egypt,
> there is none who does not arrive in it.
> As to the time of deeds on earth,
> It is the occurence of a dream;
> One says: 'Welcome safe and sound',
> To him who reaches the west [the land of the dead].

Then the coffin and the possessions of the dead person were taken down into the burial chamber which had long since been prepared in splendid style so that the dead might 'live for ever'.

Many of the people of Deir el Medineh survived undisturbed in their tombs overlooking the village until the cemetery was dug up by tomb robbers and archeologists during the last two centuries. The archeologists discovered that the oldest tombs were chambers running off vertical shafts cut into the soft shale and gravels of the hillside. Later this arrangement was changed and the burial chambers were much enlarged. Inside these crumbling caverns, excavated in the soft rock, little rooms of mud brick

Four bearers carry the encoffined body of the priest Amenemonet down into his burial chamber. After the elaborate ceremonial it is left to rest on its bier (right), and a part of the spirit of the dead man, a bird with a human head, hovers over the coffin. From a scene painted in Amenemonet's tomb close to the ancient village of Deir el Medineh

were then built, each with beautifully vaulted ceilings. It is these plastered mud brick walls and ceilings that were so beautifully decorated by the villagers, and in many cases, they have survived in a splendid state of preservation, the colours as fresh as the day they were painted.

The tomb of Sennejem, a simple necropolis worker who lived with his family in a house next to his father, Khabekhnet, in the southwestern corner of the village, is one of the best preserved and one of the most splendidly decorated. On the wall opposite the low entrance to the burial chamber Sennejem had a magnificent figure of Osiris painted. The god reminds us that we are entering the underworld. Above him two great eyes look out into the world – the 'looking glass' image of the connection between the living and the dead. Osiris' figure stands in his mummy wrappings, white

The fine figure of Osiris in his shrine, painted in the burial chamber of the tomb of Sennejem

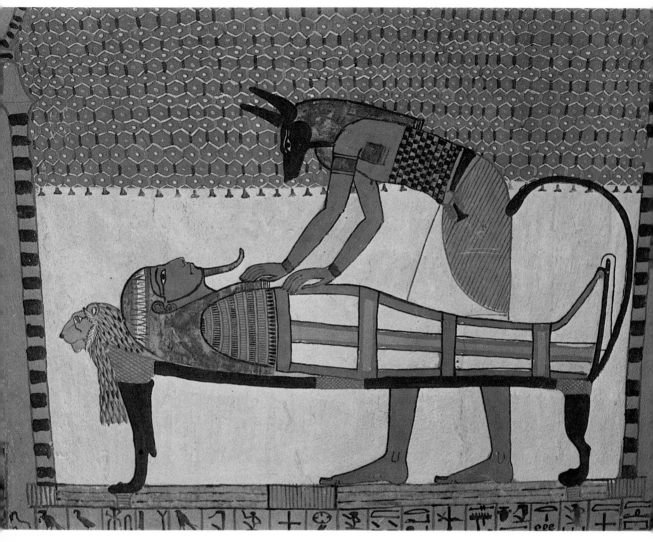

Sennejem's mummy receives the final attentions of the embalmer;
from a scene on the wall of his burial chamber

in a white-sided shrine. A lively line, drawn around the god is, in reality, just a brown line on a white panel but it describes the shape of the god so skilfully that you can believe that it has the form and volume of his figure. By Osiris' side stand two flayed jackal skins, hanging from sticks and filled with milk, the lifegiving liquid of Hathor used during the 'Opening of the Mouth'. Anubis, the jackal god that was servant and protector of the dead, also appears in these paintings as Sennejem's embalmer, tenderly putting his wrappings in their proper order as the mummy lies on its lion-headed embalming couch. During the ceremonies of mummification the chief official wore a jackal mask to represent the presence of this sleek black god.

Much of the skill that is on show on the walls of the royal tombs is also employed in these smaller paintings but here it has a casual vigour not permissible in the formal setting of the royal tombs. The canopy of Sennejem's funeral tent, for example, is decorated with the elaborate pattern and tassels that, in the kings' tombs, are employed by the same draughtsmen for the dresses of the goddesses. Even the scale of these decorations, unusually large for such small chambers, is typical of the drawings in the great halls of the royal tombs.

Most of the scenes in Sennejem's burial chamber are of him and his family worshipping the gods of a tradition that stood slightly apart from the official faith of the state. This tradition, bedded in the popular life of ancient Egypt, was concerned more with deities that daily affected the lives of ordinary people; an expression of personal piety rather than a recitation of state formulae. Given that the people of Deir el Medineh were educated in the perfect forms of the state religion, we may assume that their humbler counterparts, the endless generations of peasants who made up the bulk of the ancient Egyptian race, had a simpler, more immediate, even perhaps, a more superstitious faith.

As Sennejem lay in his brightly coloured burial chamber, with his wife and, later, his descendents, his spirit could easily move into the paintings that showed him in the afterlife. Here the quarrier of tombs is shown working the land, reaping, ploughing and tending a great orchard of fruit and flowers. As the modern inhabitants of Thebes enjoy photographs of alpine landscapes, all snow and ice, so in his day Sennejem looked forward in his paintings to a lush life in green fields working the damp fertile soil – a far cry from the dusty desert village where he and his family had lived for generations.

The fields in which the dead worked were just one location of the many afterlives that even kings could look forward to. Small figures placed in the tombs represented magical labourers who would work in the afterlife in the place of the dead person.

> Oh you ushabti [the name given to these figures], if the Osiris Sennejem is called to work in the underworld, to till the fields, to irrigate the banks or to transport sand from east to west; since hardships come in the course of such duties, if, at any time I am called, say 'behold I am present' to do the work in the dead man's place.

So might run a typical example of one of the texts that were often written on these figurines that stand in the pose of Osiris but, instead of holding the crook and the flail, that great god's symbols as ruler of the underworld, these small servants hold a basket and hoe, the perennial equipment of the Egyptian labourer.

At Deir el Medineh, however, there were few people who continually performed such heavy labours. Apart from quarrying the royal tombs, which took a year or so at the beginning of each new reign – a process of cutting away the soft limestone that easily splits if it is struck in the right way – most of the work consisted of sculpting and painting the walls and ceilings. Although their working week of ten days was a long one – and while the men were working in the royal underworld they were segregated in special compounds close to the royal valley – they had frequent holidays and were, generally, a well-cared for section of the royal establishment.

At the beginning of the New Kingdom it seems that Deir el Medineh was a small settlement of about twenty compact housing units erected on the site of earlier buildings. By the time of Ramesses III, the builder of the temple of Medinet Habu, the village had quadrupled in size and the villagers were engaged in making tombs not only in the Valley of the Kings but also in the Valley of the Queens. At the same time they may also have made some private tomb chapels for the nobles and government officials, and run small enterprises manufacturing coffins and other funerary equipment.

But this was no ordinary economy, like a Chelsea or St Ives of artist craftsmen making a good living upon the fringe of a commercial society. The Deir el Medineh workers were titled 'the Servants in the Place of Truth' and were an essential component of a society that functioned without any of the economic systems that are essential to the modern world. It was a society in which there was generally very little social movement, where the land or the state provided an ample living and where the esteem of one's neighbours and personal prestige were the most important goals. Thus the thousands of records of commercial agreements inside the village community of Deir el Medineh show a remarkable lack of exactitude about the value, quantity and quality of the goods exchanged, for these were not the prime consideration of these agreements. But casualness never extends to the record of the social contract that was being made by the parties to these agreements: buyer, seller and witnesses are always carefully listed and, sometimes, even their lineage is given.

All this, of course, made good sense in terms of the society in which these people lived. If you were a part-time varnisher of coffins or a carver of pestles working in this little community, you would have varnished and carved until you died and although people would 'buy' your products from you in barter, neither you nor your 'customers' would have attempted to 'get rich' by these transactions. In a village where the modern conceptions of freedom and commerce had no reality – where no one strove to change an inherited lifestyle which they believed was a part of the god-ordered system of creation – the modern dynamic of incentive was largely removed. Although Egyptian society in the New Kingdom was sufficiently elastic to permit the rise of people from the position of provincial scribes to holders

Sennejem and Iyneferti, his wife, worship the Gods of the Underworld.
The principal scene on one of the end walls of the vault over his
burial chamber

of some of the highest offices in the administration it would be wrong to seize on these rare instances as examples of the normal rules of ancient behaviour. In common with many other societies, the ancient Egyptians were not spurred on by promises of personal advancement or gain.

It seems probable that in the village of Deir el Medineh, real riches were closer to the biblical conception of a good life; a secure existence inside the community that might be disrupted only by envy or covetousness: the two ingredients that, in the East, are now symbolized as the Evil Eye but, in the West, have become dynamic principles of society. In this sense, the community of this little village was light years away from modern visions of society and what it can and cannot be.

Yet, as the ancient Egyptian song tells us, 'All living things breathe the air, give birth to children at the appointed time, then go to their tomb', and if you walk down the main street at Deir el Medineh you can still almost feel the life that the tiny dwellings once held. These houses, all so similar in their plan, were designed in close-knit blocks rather than the freely developed architecture of farms and villas that were built with space around them to permit buildings to be added as and when they were required. Here the tight-packed houses standing either side of the main street, reflected the organization of the work in the royal tombs which had gangs of the right and the left.

The narrow main street, its side walls perforated with the doorways of the small houses, must have been crammed with people at certain times – when the donkey convoys arrived with the village water, when the workmen returned from their work in the Valley of the Kings, or on feast days when the villagers left their houses to eat a meal by the tombs' chapels on the western hill.

The plan of the houses was much the same. The first room, at a level lower than the main street that gave access to it, held a small shrine perhaps decorated with figures of the popular household gods: Bes the dancing dwarf, Taurit the goddess of childbirth, and other such figures. Inside, these shrines were little statues of gods and, quite possibly, 'ancestor' busts that reflected the continuing power and benevolence of dead relatives. This 'reception' room gave access to another which had a single column in its centre to support the roof of palm logs and rushes that was covered with mud and stone chippings to keep the sun's heat at bay. This room, the centre of the household had a dais of mud brick that held the chair of the head of the family. Frequently it also contained a mud brick bench that had rush matting spread on it and was used both as a sofa and as a bed – a divan. The rooms behind were used for storage and cooking and a flight of stairs gave access to the roof where, it is to be imagined, the whole family slept during the hot summer nights.

Running down into the soft shale of the floor of each house were caves where supplies and provisions could be stored. In the baking heat of the enclosed desert valley such shade and cool as could be obtained was essential for the preservation of food and drink. Conversely, the bread ovens, which were a source of great heat, were placed either along the outer walls of the village or partly buried among the loose rocks of the mountainside. The ovens, which were common to almost every house were similar to those still used in Egyptian villages today. When they are used to bake loaves of fresh local flour it is the finest bread that you can eat. Ancient loaves, looking the same as their modern counterparts, are occasionally found during excavations and often look uncannily fresh. The ancient Egyptians must have been great connoisseurs of bread, for more than forty different varieties are known to us.

By modern standards the village houses are very small and, like many peoples who flourish in hot climates, the villagers probably lived mainly in the open air. Domestic groups were small – not the large extended families of many African societies – and similar in size to the nuclear family unit. Words like 'son' and 'brother' were also used to describe other relationships, such as cousins and lovers. Among the scraps of writing that have survived, many intimate details of the ancient lives are recorded. They describe quick-tempered and patient individuals, honest and corrupt foremen, adulteries, rows, love, noisy families, the loneliness of bereavement, of concern and pride in family and children – altogether a very wide span of the emotions of family life.

Complementing these remarkable documents, the extraordinary wealth of the physical remains from the village tell us a great deal about material life there. A man's sandals, taken from his tomb, may show us how he walked; the remains of his meal show us something of his diet. Their musical instruments, furniture, linens, clothes – sometimes still dirty and stained – all have been preserved. Small scenes, drawn, like the texts, on potsherds and flakes of stone show us the delights of their lives, of dancing, of acrobatic entertainers, of caricatures and satires, of lovers knotted in languorous embraces.

But life at Deir el Medineh was not all beer and skittles. There were times when the administration failed to provide the villagers' supplies and they were forced to stop work on the royal tomb and come down from the desert to the offices of the administration to protest about their neglect. These demonstrations have been called the first strikes in history but they are a far cry from the manifestations of organized labour operating in a modern economy. Nevertheless, there is strong evidence that the community quickly appreciated the effect of the massed appearances at the offices of the administration.

The best reported of many incidents, which was, perhaps, the first to take place, describes what happened towards the end of the reign of Ramesses III : '. . . today the gang of workmen have passed by the walls of the royal tomb saying: we are hungry, 18 days of this month have already

gone by, and they sat down behind the funerary temple of Tuthmosis III.' Representatives of the management then appeared and attempted to get the workers to return to the Valley of the Kings. 'Return! We have a message from the Pharaoh. But the workmen remained in the same place all day.' Perhaps they had heard these pleas before and were not impressed by them. After more days of similar events, the villagers asked a scribe and some priests of one of the royal mortuary temples to write a letter direct to the king on their behalf. For, as they said: 'We have come here driven by hunger and thirst. We have no clothes, no fat, no fish and no vegetables. Write this to the king, our good lord, so that we may be given the means to live'.

Here the papyrus ends. But the villagers' protest must have been successful, for the life of their community flourished for another hundred years. What is particularly interesting about these events is the way in which the villagers apparently realized the effectiveness of their actions. For, in another strike, a spokesman had this to say to the administration: 'It was not hunger that made us pass by the walls [of the king's tomb on which they worked] but we have serious complaints to make: truly scandalous things have happened in this place of pharaoh!'

This is a statement of people responding to what they consider to be an immoral situation with a public display of dissatisfaction that employed the same type of protest that had earlier taken place in attempts to obtain their food rations, 'so that we might live'. Here, perhaps, we may detect the beginnings of civic awareness. This small community, far from the normal agrarian society of Egypt, produced, it seems, most unusual men.

Vaulted storerooms on the north side of the mortuary temple of Ramesses II, the largest of more than a hundred similar structures that once surrounded the temple. Such warehouses were a common feature of all mortuary-temple complexes at Thebes and it has been estimated that just one of them, filled to a depth of one metre with grain, could have supplied the needs of the population of the village at Deir el Medineh for a year

CHAPTER TWELVE

ALEXANDER'S BAND

It is, however, in the official works of the royal artists that we may see the public side of the ancient Egyptian face. These works are stamped with an extraordinary confidence and aesthetic command. No one today, can make such effortlessly beautiful statuary of comparable proportions – we just do not possess the subtle group sensitivities required to work on such enormous projects with that sort of precision or unity of style. They have the individuality of an age-old civilization secure in its values.

Politically, however, the days of the New Kingdom were numbered, and it came to its end around 1000 B.C. – an event that followed a hundred-year period of very low water levels in the East African lake system that was probably reflected in equally low Nile flood levels. Along with other considerations, the transference of the court from the narrow strip of Upper Egypt to the broad wet Delta plain was, doubtless, a sensible political response to harsh ecological reality.

So, as the centre of national culture withdrew from the Nile Valley to the north so, increasingly, Egyptian society became a part of the wider community of the nations of the Middle East – in Asia Minor, in Greece, in Palestine and the Lebanon. The Egyptian kings led a political existence that was far removed from the society of their predecessors. At times their armies were composed almost entirely of foreign mercenaries. The country was filled with new preoccupations and new ideals. The trappings of the ancient Nilotic civilization became the ornaments of a new society.

For some 600 years, ten dynasties of kings built their capitals on the damp Delta soil. It is easy to see the attractions of such sites: even the New Kingdom monarchs had brought the patterns of exuberant Delta foliage to the palaces and temples of Thebes. Today many of the Delta cities are but huge earthen mounds sliced away by peasants and archeologists alike. Nearby lie great piles of granite blocks, ruined temples made of stones and filled with statuary brought from the old sites of the Valley.

Alexander the Great, dressed as king of Egypt, worships Amun in scenes cut in relief on the outside wall of the god's sanctuary at the Temple of Luxor

From the end of the New Kingdom until the arrival of Alexander and the Macedonian armies in 332 B.C., the surviving political records of Egypt have all the incoherent charm of a tattered copy of Wisden. But even more fascinating are the arts of this diffuse era, for if you look at the reliefs and sculptures of the Late Period and compare them with those of the New Kingdom, you may detect processes of change, of transformation – perhaps, disintegration would be a better word – taking place before your eyes.

From the very beginning of Egypt's religious traditions, the Delta was seen as the mysterious primeval swamp where Horus had spent his childhood, a dense green marsh, a landscape that was not defined like the clear, two-dimensional space of the Nile Valley. Now, in the Late Period with the court removed from the narrow world of Upper Egypt to the Delta, new sensibilities were aroused in the artists that led to the creation of a rounded and more volumetric style of representation, and as this new awareness of internal space developed, the artists' age-old sensitivity to the flat surface of the walls on which they worked was lost. And once this flat surface was penetrated – as it was in Renaissance Europe by the first perspective diagrams of the Italian artists – it was as if it had been pricked and burst: the artists had realized a new style and could no longer return in innocence to the traditional conventions of their art.

This very individual use of space in both painting and relief had always been one of the most distinctive qualities of the traditional state art. The figures all exist inside a fragile envelope of space that is contained on the surface of the wall. Inside this world, every element of the scene, both figure and ground, are linked together like the words on this printed page. Here the ink seems to occupy a space which dances just a little above the actual surface of the paper and it is inside a similar envelope of space, that much of Egyptian art is held. Just as when you read this page you see more than the printer's ink and the shapes of the letters, so the traditional 'thin' space of the Egyptian artists easily held many different worlds of meaning. There was simply no need for vanishing point, perspectives, or spatial illusions, for an acute sensibility to surface and a thin flat space held all the potential that they required of their literary/visual art.

Today, it is important to guard against looking at this ancient art with eyes that are too modern; to guard against filling the gaps between figures and hieroglyphs in the way that we 'read' the electronic patterns on a television screen or a black-and-white image of a photograph. These modern images rarely hold the different levels of meaning that are present in the careful constructions of the ancient 'pictures'. The style and content of an ancient Egyptian 'picture' (which is what we make of the ancient art when we display it in loose panels in museums or in the rectangular illustrations of books) is far more highly charged and deliberately made, like the work of a composer of orchestral music.

A certain Amenhotep, High Priest of Amun at the Temple of Karnak during the late Twentieth Dynasty, receiving honours from King Ramesses IX. Although the figures in this relief (in the Temple of Karnak) show a new and very lively sense of form the hieroglyphs seem to have lost all connection with them

We may see the beginnings of this dissolution of the traditional space of Egyptian art as early as the Twentieth Dynasty, when the hieroglyphs that accompany the figures on the temple walls begin to stand apart from them. The acute sensitivities that enabled the artist to hold everything in inter-relationship on the wall's surface began to dissolve and that 'thin' space slipped through his fingers.

Not surprisingly, it was also at this time that large numbers of cast-bronze sculptures were made, some of which are large and lavish. Many are also exceptionally well modelled and show varieties of pose that could not be achieved with the traditional techniques of stone sculpture.

This unusually vigorous sculpture was probably intended to be cast in bronze. It shows Ramesses XI worshipping the goddess Ma'at, and is from his tomb in the Valley of the Kings; made of beeswax it is just 14.5 cm high

*Relief showing bearers bringing offerings to the tomb of Ibi, Chief
Steward of the ruler of Thebes during the Twenty-fifth Dynasty.
The sculptors have carefully copied their figures from others in
Hatshepsut's temples – reliefs that were already some seven hundred
years old!*

The bronze figures stand freely in space with their arms outstretched and
often the crowns that they wear stand boldly away from them with a
naturalism that is quite new. Some of these bronzes are overlaid with a
rich surface pattern of inlaid gold and silver which emphasizes the novel
roundness of their forms.

This is a very new art for Egypt, for it is an art of addition, of modelling
up the figure from a thin core using hot wax that will later be cast in
bronze. It is a process of *adding* more shape to a form, a process of slow
enlargement. Traditional Egyptian stone carving, on the other hand, had
been made with pounding stones and soft copper chisels, and was an art

201

of *subtraction*, of pounding a block *down* to size. The introduction of iron chisels during the Late Period changed this heavy bruising process and gave the sculptor a sharp strong tool with which he could virtually draw in three dimensions, working quickly into the soft stone. So, although many of the masterpieces of the Late Period were still made in the traditional way, artists now knew that there was a choice.

Working against the new and robust sense of form there were several attempts to return to the old ways: deliberate imitations of past styles. Figures were copied from older monuments, such as Hatshepsut's Temple or from Old and Middle Kingdom tombs. At Thebes during the Twenty-fifth and Twenty-sixth Dynasties the work in the tomb chapels made for the officials, who then governed Egypt, was sometimes organized like an academy of art. In some of these tombs every figure on the wall is different, some finished roughly, others made with immense care as both artists and pupils try to perfect their craft. In other tombs of this era, these same hard-won skills are tested on huge areas of wall that unfold, layer after layer, deep into the limestone in a dangerous succession of passages, tunnels and secret entrances. These tombs are as much compendiums of Egyptian funerary beliefs as they are of art and architectural styles. All the texts and architecture of the royal and private monuments have been added together to make the largest tombs in Egypt and, probably, the most elaborate funerary monuments in the world. In a sense these are the Victorian monuments of ancient Egypt, massive conglomerations of style and form that, in their sum, have made a new aesthetic, a new art.

Yet, in small pieces, on slabs of stone plundered for museums or collectors, the extraordinary reliefs from these tombs are often difficult to tell apart from the works of earlier periods that the artists were trying to emulate. In larger panels, however, the new sophistications, the deliberate grasping after simplicity, becomes obvious, just as does the attempt to hold that fragile envelope of space on the surface of the wall – the same space that earlier, less sophisticated artists controlled with such panache. Like the Victorian arts, this, apparently, is new wine in old bottles – rather thin and very conscientious. But if you taste it carefully you will find that in reality it is quite a different beverage.

This same spirit of antiquarianism also resulted in the excavation of the tombs of the Umm el Ga'ab at Abydos. There, one of the First Dynasty royal tombs was identified as the tomb of Osiris and carefully restored. Then, a splendid black schist statue of the dead god was placed in the centre of the ancient burial chamber showing Osiris lying on his embalming table with Isis, the bird, hovering over him during the magical engendering of Horus.

At Sakkara, too, other ancient archeologists penetrated the heart of Djoser's Step Pyramid, quarrying new and elaborate galleries that ran right to its centre. At this time the remains of King Djoser were probably rediscovered, carefully restored, and reburied by these pious tunnellers, digging back far into their own past. Likewise at Giza, the pyramids of the Fourth Dynasty were entered once again, and one of the plundered kings they found, was reburied in his sarcophagus inside a big rounded wooden coffin typical of the Late Period style.

What an incredible artistic legacy ancient Egypt eventually bequeathed to the world! Numerous architectural elements have directly entered the Western tradition – the stone arch, the fluted column, indeed, an entire language in stone. The basis of Western sculptural form, our image of the human figure is also ultimately derived from Egyptian traditions. Greek *kouroi* figures, for example, were measured in canons derived from Egyptian prototypes and were usually posed in the manner of Egyptian standing statues; the first known Egyptian figure – that of a First Dynasty king from Sakkara – also shares this same pose. But, apart from this long list of forms and iconography, the most important legacy was technique – the knowledge based on thousands of years of working in a single tradition that enabled the less proficient artists of younger cultures to advance in relatively short periods of time. When Greek scholars said that they had been trained in their subjects by Egyptian priests at Memphis they were not describing an archaic polytechnic that they had attended but were acknowledging the existence of an enormous substratum of knowledge – of experience and tradition, of technique and attainment – on which all the new cultures of the Mediterranean had freely drawn: Egypt was father to them all.

During the late Period, Egypt was repeatedly invaded: first by Nubians, then by Assyrians, and then by Persians, and finally, the Macedonian Greeks. The Assyrians did the most damage. Unlike the Nubian kings who had piously attempted to restore parts of the traditional order of Egypt, the Assyrians came to plunder. At Thebes they carted away all the gold and the other treasures of the temples, and you may still see the blackened shattered jambs and lintels of the great pylon doors that they fired during a general sacking and plundering. In 332 B.C. Alexander the Great arrived in Egypt and, after his campaign of conquest, spent some time with the temple priests whose descriptions of the traditional powers and prerogatives of Pharaoh, it has been suggested, started the young king on the path of world conqueror. Alexander was returning to the fountain head of his national traditions: good Greek learning was replaced by a Middle Eastern attitude to kingship and divinity.

The foreign kings who stayed long enough in Egypt to rule the country had all taken on the role of Pharaoh, and Alexander did so with great enthusiasm. The sanctuary of the temple at Luxor, built in New Kingdom times, was replaced by a new building which was decorated with reliefs in the traditional manner, showing the Macedonian kitted-out like an Egyptian king, his name spelled laboriously in hieroglyphics. Similarly, Alexander's successor built a new sanctuary for Amun-Re at Karnak and Alexander's general, Ptolemy, who succeeded to rule, continued to play Pharaoh and to honour the ancient gods.

This was hardly immoral. There was nothing in their Hellenistic religion that preached of the exclusivity of any deity and, indeed, this honouring of the native gods would have been seen as both a sensitive and a pious act. Nor was this all a one-way traffic; three hundred years earlier an Egyptian king had dedicated his battle armour at a shrine in Greece. It was natural, therefore, that the dynasty of Ptolemies that the general founded should continue those traditions and, indeed, that it not only recognized all the Egyptian deities but also amalgamated the identities of several gods. Later in this process of giving and taking gods – similar exchanges took place throughout the Hellenistic world – the cult of Isis spread first through the Mediterranean and then, during the Roman Empire, into France, Britain and Germany. It also seems that certain of the goddess's attributes were later assimilated into the cult of the Virgin Mary.

General Ptolemy's greatest invention was a god that was a mixture of Osiris and the Apis bull (an animal cult which had gained particular favour during the Late Period at Memphis) and this odd figure, a sort of Zeus, was named Serapis. This cross-cultural god was particularly revered in Alexandria, the great coastal city on the edge of the western Delta, that had been founded by Alexander, and was now the Ptolemaic capital of Egypt.

Egypt now entered the last phases of its independent history – albeit under Macedonian rule – with a cultural heritage intact and with a strong and prosperous government. In the Nile Valley the Ptolemies inaugurated a new and splendid era. The Macedonians brought strong local government along with many of the alien institutions of the Greek world to the remotest villages of Egypt. Gymnasia were built in the larger towns; mummies of the period were sometimes buried with manuscripts of Homer and other Greek writers. Despite the well-regulated prosperity of this harsh foreign rule the nationalist Thebans revolted time and time again and it was during one of those occasions that the mortuary temple of Tuthmosis III was quite destroyed. But the Ptolemies were great builders, greater perhaps, than those of any other single age. Right through the three-hundred-year span of their dynasty the stone quarries were heavily worked and building continued at Karnak and many other sites on a scale at least as large as anything that had gone before. A recent count of Ptolemaic temples in Egypt that have survived in one form or another runs, literally, into thousands.

In many of the provincial centres of Upper Egypt, the small temples of earlier times were demolished and new, crisply made stone monuments erected in their place. Unlike the rougher-hewn masonry of earlier periods, these Ptolemaic temples were built with a care and thoroughness that had not been equalled for thousands of years. At Karnak it was the Ptolemies alone who were able to complete the construction of the final, huge pylon at the temple which, the ancient building scheme dictated, had to be made ever larger as the temple plan was extended down towards the river. This last pylon is larger and better made than many of the pyramids.

Equally impressive are the temples of the other Egyptian provinces, at

A granite relief of Philip Arrhidaeus, half brother of Alexander the Great, offering lettuces to Amun. It is carved on the outer walls of the god's sanctuary – built at Philip's orders – in the Temple of Karnak

*Sunset at the Temple of Kom Ombo, which was dedicated to a
mixture of Egyptian and Hellenistic gods*

Esna, Kom Ombo, Denderah and Edfu, and these have furnished the West
with powerful and dignified visions of ancient Egypt. They are the
monuments of the age of both Cleopatra and Cecil B. De Mille, a splendid
hybrid of the ancient art. But although these buildings are some of the
most popular attractions for visitors, they are frequently maligned by
specialists who have described them as caricatures of older work: ancient
Egypt vulgarized and misinterpreted. The Ptolemaic reliefs, especially,
have been described as travesties of the ancient art, works that 'flatter only
to deceive'!

There is, however, little point in judging these new arts by the standards
of their forerunners. For, if you look carefully at the smooth well-made

206

Ptolemaic hieroglyphs in the Temple of Kom Ombo

The Temple of Hathor, Lady of Denderah. The building was begun during the time of the Ptolemaic kings and completed under the Roman emperors

reliefs that cover these great temples' walls you will find something quite fresh; something that is neither a return to the old ways nor an attempt to surpass that work by sheer technical skill. This is a genuinely new art. The artists had somehow rediscovered the surface of the wall on which they worked; once again they were able to compose their scenes with a confidence not seen since New Kingdom times. It is a vigorous art, and how the old figures have been changed! Elaborate compositions, extraordinarily decorated hieroglyphics, and a roundness and fullness of form that has, at last, been held in balance with the surface of the wall. And it is the more extraordinary for that. For, if you close your eyes and run your hands over the reliefs you will feel the difference: it has a *reality* of form, a veracity of shape which, though at first glance may appear strained or inflated, *feels* correct and quite reasonable to the touch. It is a sensuous art that has regained the earlier confidence by concentrating once more on the inner forms of the subject, on the reality of a hand or a foot as experienced from within as a living thing. This had been a major characteristic of the great ages of the earlier art and one that had enabled the artist to bring his subject to life within the thin space of the wall's surface. It was a part of the joyful celebration of life that the artists had regained. Yet these Ptolemaic reliefs are completely different from the old arts: more hedonistic, more sensual, more earthly.

The architecture, too, is equally remarkable and equally extravagant.

As their predecessors had tunnelled into the centre of the Step Pyramid so these Ptolemaic architects burrowed about in the traditional architectural forms of the New Kingdom to re-invent the ancients' architecture. As they built their great temples – and rather better than their predecessors had done – they opened out the normally solid masses and replaced them with screen walls and columned halls. And deep underneath the temples they burrowed an elaborate series of passageways which penetrated the heavy structures like holes in cheese. Pylons, too, were riddled with extra passages, stairs, rooms and corridors.

The traditional temple complex now became an elaborate rationalized liturgical machine whose functions may still be understood from the texts carved into its walls. In their zeal the Ptolemaic artists and architects not only rescued the ancient arts of drawing, but also made their temples so perfectly ordered that, as one scholar has observed, if there were no other monuments left in Egypt we should still be able to reconstruct the ancient faith and its ceremonies from their texts, wall scenes, and architecture. In earlier temples the daily rituals of the cult are usually described in the texts and wall reliefs in a diffuse way; the priests saw the daily rituals as continuing for ever. But in the Ptolemaic temples all is carefully labelled and displayed on the walls. They have been described as sanctuaries where the ancient religion was most carefully maintained: centres of national resistance facing the advance of Hellenism.

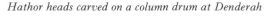

Hathor heads carved on a column drum at Denderah

At the centre of these temples in dark sandstone halls, the great granite monoliths of the gods' sanctuaries stood glinting like polished silver. All around them were the rooms of the gods' treasuries, the perfume and incense manufactures, halls for the statues of other gods, rooms for the storage of ritual equipment, rooms for sacred emblems, and libraries of liturgical and religious texts. And in these complex buildings regiments of priests kept the ritual offices functioning as precisely as a power station.

At the Temple of Denderah, the beautiful House of Hathor that stood screened behind huge mud brick walls amid the fields of Upper Egypt, priests performed mysterious rites in hidden holy chambers and appeared, later, on the temple's roof overlooking both the fields and the river; there they announced with splendid display and processional that the powers of the gods would once more fructify Egypt. At Edfu and Kom Ombo similar rites were conducted with other gods.

To walk around these temples today is a strange experience. You wonder why the priests are not still there, why the buildings are deserted.

What happened, of course, was that the Ptolemaic Empire came under the control of Rome: the last Ptolemy, a child of Julius Caesar and Cleopatra, was murdered on the orders of Emperor Augustus and Egypt was made into the emperor's private estate. The country was run like a huge farm, its grain sent to Rome. Egypt, which a thousand years before had turned away from the enclosed world of the Nile Valley to join the cultures of the Mediterranean, had finally been engulfed by that single force that had overrun the entire classical world.

Under Roman rule work continued on the temples of Upper Egypt, but on a lesser scale; and indeed some of the Roman emperors built small monuments of their own. From all over the Empire tourists came to see the ancient monuments, to visit Thebes and the realms of Memnon, to wonder at the city of Alexandria which the Ptolemies had made into one of the most elegant and educated in the world. But the Romans were never really at home with the cultures of their eastern colonies. The relaxed hedonism, the cheerful acceptance of all gods, the basing of private morality on public standing were the antithesis of the values of the Roman patricians. But slowly and surely, the strict moralities of Rome were themselves overwhelmed by those of the east that they had captured by force of arms. Along with the gods of Syria and Asia Minor, Isis came to Rome and eventually one of these eastern religions, Christianity, took control of the empire. In Egypt it brought more destruction than had the Assyrians. After millenia of adaption and transformation, ancient Egypt was shattered, and then, finally, destroyed. This is why the ancient temples stand today as clean as empty sea shells: the shock of Christianity was sudden and complete.

The huge Hypostyle Hall of Denderah temple

Christ's religion was first brought to Egypt by St Mark the Evangelist and for three centuries after that time the converts to the new faith suffered appalling persecution at the hands of the Romans. The so-called Gospel of the pseudo-Matthew – one not included in the modern Bible – describes a part of the visit of the Holy Family in Egypt as they fled south from Herod's soldiers. Many Egyptians believe that the Holy Family travelled far into the Nile Valley, turning around in their journey at Assiut, where, for a while, they lived in the tombs of the Middle Kingdom monarchs of that ancient city. Today, thousands of pilgrims come to a church close to these tombs to worship at this holy site.

It is, perhaps, suitably symbolic that the Holy Family took over and inhabited an ancient tomb at Assiut, for in their journey through Egypt they continually confronted the ancient gods and the child Jesus invariably drove them from their temples. At one city the ancient statues cried out when they saw the child : 'this is the King!'. In a market, whose busy streets were too narrow for his mother to pass, Jesus, performing a juvenile miracle, turned the camel trains to stone and, in so doing appropriated the ancient avenues of sphinxes that line the approaches to some of the ancient temples for Christianity!

As Jesus combatted the ancient gods with stronger magic, so the ferocity of the Christian converts towards the ancient monuments betrays a deep belief in their continuing power. When, in fourth century Alexandria, a huge mob of Christians converged on the great temple of Serapis – regarded by a contemporary, after some six hundred and fifty years of worship, as being the 'one and only new sight in the world' – they were not only out to destroy the images of paganism but they were also in great fear of their lives :

> But the pagans themselves had spread abroad a conviction that if a man's hand was laid upon that image [of the god], the earth would straightaway yawn open and dissolve into formlessness, and the sky would suddenly fall headlong. For a while this kept the people paralysed until one of the soldiers, fortified more by his faith than by his armour, seized an axe, and rising with all his strength, dashed it against the jaw of the deceiver. Christians and pagans shouted aloud, but the sky did not fall or the earth subside.

Also in Alexandria, the renowned teacher Hypatia, a daughter of the mathematician Theon and a famous neo-Platonist philosopher, was torn to pieces by a mob encouraged by Bishop, later St, Cyril. Another bishop, burning temples and houses alike for the greater glory of God, raided a village in the Delta and burnt not only its temple and more than three hundred of its gods, but also the High Priest. The Christians who, earlier,

Sunlight slanting through the doorway of the First Pylon of the
Temple of Amun-Re at Karnak

had themselves been the victims of fire and venom now returned their torments in kind. Not until the arrival of the Europeans during the last century did the ancient monuments suffer so much.

Nowhere, perhaps, is the furious terror of these attacks more apparent than in the great temple of Hathor at Denderah, though in fact, there is hardly a temple in Egypt that does not bear the marks of the Christians' flat copper chisels, running deeply and quickly across the ancient reliefs, cutting the feared images into harmless fragments. At Denderah they must have erected scaffolding to reach the full extent of the broad high walls and from these platforms they attacked the wall scenes one after another as conscientiously as the avenging agents of Tuthmosis III had attacked the figures of Hatshepsut some seventeen centuries before. But this time there were no pious pagans left to restore the mutilated reliefs and we must be grateful, therefore, that these Christians did not care to finish their work and that some of the reliefs are still unmarked.

Even the frenzied chiselling of the Hathor-headed column tops that stand like marvellous totem poles in the gloom of the Denderah temple's first court, have not destroyed the Great Lady's identity. The vast building holds its sanctity to this day, much to the wonderment of modern tourists, who mostly believe that they have come to see a picturesque ruin. In the last century, before the Suez Canal was cut, Indian Army troops passed by Denderah on their march from the Red Sea to Alexandria, a part of the long journey from Calcutta to Portsmouth. Much to the amazement of their British officers, the Sepoys identified the huge images of Hathor as one of their own Hindu gods, and worshipped in the great empty temple.

In the first pages of this book there is a quotation from Hermes Trismegistus, another Alexandrian deity linked with Thoth. The passage was the beginning of a prophecy by this god and now, perhaps, it is fitting to continue the words of this ancient sage:

Do you not know, O Asclepius, that Egypt is the copy of Heaven, or rather, the place where here below are mediated and projected all operations which govern and actuate the heavenly forces? Even more than that, if the whole truth is to be told, our land is the temple of the entire World. Nevertheless, since it is fitting that wise men should have foreknowledge of all things, you should not be unacquainted with this. There will be a time when it will be manifest that it was in vain that the Egyptians cherished godhead with pious will and constant devotion, and all holy reverence for the gods will vanish and be made of no effect. Godhead will go back from earth to heaven. Egypt will be abandoned, and the land which was the home of worship will be stripped of the presence of the deities and left bare. Foreigners will fill this region and the land; and there will be not only a neglect of devotions but, what is harder, religion, piety and divine worship will be banned as by law under stated penalty. Then this most holy land, the abode of shrines and temples, will be most full of graves and of dead men.

PEOPLE AND PLACES

PERIOD	KINGS NAMED IN TEXT	DYNASTY	DATES OF RULE (B.C.)	INDIVIDUALS NAMED IN TEXT
Archaic	Narmer	1	c. 3100–?	
	Djet-Hor	1	c. 3000–?	
	Khasekhemui	2	2703–2686	
	Djoser	3	2667–2648	Imhotep
Old Kingdom	Sneferu	4	2613–2589	Nefermaat
	Cheops	4	2589–2566	
	Mycerinos	4	c. 2528–2500	Debhen
	Sahure	5	2487–2473	
	Unas	5	2375–2345	Ptah-hotep
	Teti	6	2345–2333	Mereruka
	Pepi II	6	c. 2269–2175	Mekhu, Sabni, Ankhtifi (*fl. c.* 2150)
Middle Kingdom	Senusert I	12	1971–1928	
	Amenemhet III	12	1842–1797	
New Kingdom	Ahmose	18	1570–1546	Queen Ahmes Nefertiri
	Amenhotep I	18	1546–1526	
	Tuthmosis I	18	c. 1525–1512	Queen Ahmose
	,, II	18	1512–1504	Queen Isis
	Hatshepsut	18	1503–1482	Princess Neferure, Senmut, Hapuseneb
	Tuthmosis III	18	1504–1450	
	Amenhotep III	18	1417–1379	
	Akhenaten	18	c. 1379–1362	
	Seti I	19	1318–1304	Villagers of Deir el
	Ramesses II	19	1304–1237	Medineh *fl.* throughout the New Kingdom
	Ramesses III	20	1198–1166	
	,, V	20	1160–1156	
	,, VI	20	1156–1148	
	,, IX	20	1140–1121	High Priest Amenhotep
	,, XI	20	1113–1085	
Late Period	Pianky	25	751–730	
				Ibi *fl. c.* 650
	Alexander the Great		332–323	
	Ptolemy I		304–283	
	,, XV		44–30	
	Cleopatra VII		51–30	
	Augustus		27–A.D. 14	

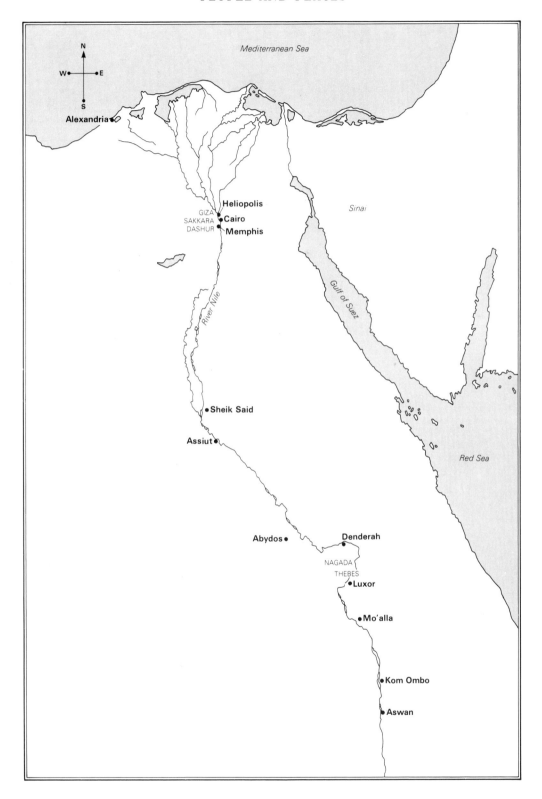

SELECT
BIBLIOGRAPHY

The following abbreviations have been used for scholarly journals:
AJA: American Journal of Archeology
JEA: Journal of Egyptian Archeology
JNES: Journal of Near Eastern Studies
MDAIK: Mitteilungen des Deutschen Archäologischen Instituts Abteilung Kairo

GENERAL

Baedeker's Egypt and the Sudan. 8th edn. Leipzig, 1929

Breasted, James Henry. *Ancient Records of Egypt*. Chicago, 1906

Butzer, Karl W. *Early Hydraulic Civilization in Egypt*. Chicago, 1976

Cambridge Ancient History. 2nd edn. Cambridge, 1964–71

Darby, William, *et al. Food : The Gift of Osiris*. London, 1977

Erman, Adolf (trans. Aylward M. Blackman). *The Literature of the Ancient Egyptians*. London, 1927

Frankfort, Henri, *et al. The Intellectual Adventure of Ancient Man*. Chicago, 1946

Gardiner, Sir Alan. *Egypt of the Pharaohs*. Oxford, 1961

Giedion, Siegfried. *The Eternal Present : The Beginnings of Architecture*. London, 1964

Groenewegen-Frankfort, Henrietta A. *Arrest and Movement*. London, 1951

Herodotus Book II (trans. W. G. Waddell). London, 1939

Lichtheim, Miriam. *Ancient Egyptian Literature*. 2 vols. Berkeley, 1973–76

Lucas, Arthur, rev. by R. Harris. *Ancient Egyptian Materials and Industries*. 4th edn. London, 1962

Porter, Rosalind, and Bertha Moss. *Topographical Bibliography of Ancient Egyptian Hieroglyphic Texts, Reliefs and Paintings*. 7 vols. Oxford, 1927–

Posener, Georges, *et al. A Dictionary of Egyptian Civilization*. London, 1962

Vandier, Jacques. *Manuel d'Archeologie Égyptienne*. 4 vols. Paris, 1952–64

CHAPTER ONE

Bell, Barbara. 'The Dark Ages in Ancient History', *AJA*, 75, 1971

Bell, Barbara. 'Climate and the History of Egypt', *AJA*, 79, 1975

Hume, W. F. *Geology of Egypt*. Cairo, 1925

Rushdi Said, *The Geology of Egypt*. New York, 1962

CHAPTER TWO

Frankfort, Henri. *Kingship and the Gods*. Chicago, 1948

Frankfort, Henri. *Ancient Egyptian Religion*. New York, 1948

Goedicke, Hans. 'Unity and Diversity in the Oldest Religion of Ancient Egypt' in *Essays of Honour of W. F. Albright*. Baltimore, 1977

Kees, Herman. *Ancient Egypt : A Cultural Topography*. London, 1961

Rundle Clark, R. T. *Myth and Symbol in the Religion of Ancient Egypt*. London, 1959

CHAPTER THREE

Ayrton, Edward R. and William L. S. Loat. *Pre-Dynastic Cemetery at El Mahasna*. London, 1911

Baumgartel, Elise J. *The Cultures of Prehistoric Egypt*. 2 vols. Oxford, 1955; 1960

Baumgartel, Elise J. *Petrie's Nagada Excavation : A Supplement*. London, 1970

de Morgan, Jacques. *Recherches sur les Origines de l'Égypte. Ethnographie Préhistorique*. Paris, 1897

Gombrich, E. H. *In Search of Cultural History*. Oxford, 1969

Kaiser, Werner. *Studien zur Vorgeschichte Ägyptens*, Vol. I. Glückstadt, 1974

Kroeber, Alfred L. *Style and Civilizations.* Berkeley, 1963

Murray, Margaret. *My First Hundred Years.* London, 1963

Naville, Édouard. *Cemeteries of Abydos,* Part I. London, 1914

Petrie, Sir William Flinders. *Nagada and Ballas.* London, 1896

Petrie, Sir William Flinders. *Diospolis Parva.* London, 1901

Petrie, Sir William Flinders. *Seventy Years in Archaeology.* London, 1933

Petrie, Sir William Flinders, with David G. Hogarth. *Koptos.* London, 1896

CHAPTER FOUR

Amélineau, Émile. *Mission Amélineau : les Nouvelles Fouilles d'Abydos.* Paris, 1895–1905

Bietak, Manfred. 'Urban Archeology and the "Town Problem" in Ancient Egypt' in *Egyptology and the Social Sciences.* Cairo, 1979

Emery, Walter B. *et al. Great Tombs of the First Dynasty.* 3 vols. Cairo and London, 1949–58

Emery, Walter B. *Archaic Egypt.* Harmondsworth, 1961

Iversen, Erik. *Canon and Proportions in Egyptian Art.* Warminster, 1975

Kemp, Barry J. 'The early development of towns in Egypt'. *Antiquity* LI. London, 1977

Petrie, Sir William Flinders. *The Royal Tombs of the First Dynasty.* 2 vols. London, 1900–1901

Petrie, Sir William Flinders. *Abydos, I.* London, 1902

Trigger, Bruce G. 'Nubian, Negro, Black, Nilotic?' in *Africa in Antiquity,* I. Brooklyn, 1978

CHAPTER FIVE

Emery, Walter B. *Archaic Egypt.* Harmondsworth, 1961

Firth, Cecil Mallaby, and James Edward Quibell. *The Step Pyramid.* 2 vols. London, 1935

Lauer, Jean-Philippe. *Histoire Monumentale des Pyramids d'Égypte.* Cairo, 1962

Ricke, Herbert. *Bemerkungen zur Ägyptischen Baukunst des Alten Reiches.* 2 vols. Cairo, 1944, 1950

CHAPTER SIX

Bennet, John. 'Pyramid Names', *JEA,* 52, 1966

Childe, Gordon. *What Happened in History.* Harmondsworth, 1942

Edwards, I. E. S. *The Pyramids of Egypt.* Harmondsworth, 1961

Lauer, Jean-Philippe. *Observations sur les Pyramides.* Cairo, 1960

Petrie, Sir William Flinders. *The Pyramids and Temples of Giza.* London, 1883

Piankoff, Alexander. *The Pyramid of Unas.* Princeton, 1968

Pound, Ezra. In Foreword to *Selected Cantos.* London, 1967

CHAPTER SEVEN

Junker, Hermann. *Grabungen auf dem Friedhof des Alten Reiches bei den Pyramiden von Gîza.* 12 parts. Vienna, 1929–55

Sakkara Expedition. *The Mastaba of Mereruka.* 2 parts. Chicago, 1938

Smith, William Stevenson. *A History of Egyptian Sculpture and Painting in the Old Kingdom.* Oxford, 1949

Smith, William Stevenson. *The Art and Architecture of Ancient Egypt.* Harmondsworth, 1965

Vandier, Jacques. *Mo'alla.* Cairo, 1950

CHAPTER EIGHT

Arnold, Dieter. *Gräber des Alten und Mittleren Reiches in El-Tarif.* Mainz, 1976

Bietak, Manfred. *Tell el Dab'a II.* Vienna, 1975

Breasted, James Henry. *A History of Egypt.* New York, 1909

Breasted, James Henry. *The Dawn of Conscience.* New York, 1933

Diop, Cheikh Anta. *The African Origin of Civilization : Myth or Reality.* Westport, 1974

Gardiner, Sir Alan. *The Kadesh Inscriptions of Ramesses II.* Oxford, 1960

Hölscher, Uvo. *The Excavation of Medinet Habu.* 5 vols. Chicago, 1934–51

Leach, Edmund. *Genesis as Myth and other Essays.* London, 1969

Nims, Charles F. *Thebes of the Pharaohs.* London, 1965

Maspero, Sir Gaston. *The Struggle of the Nations.* London, 1896

Van Seters, John. *The Hyksos : A New Investigation.* New Haven, 1966

Wilson, John. *The Burden of Egypt.* Chicago, 1951

Winlock, Herbert E. *The Rise and Fall of the Middle Kingdom in Thebes.* New York, 1947

Yadin, Yigael. *The Art of Warfare in Biblical Lands.* London, 1963

CHAPTER NINE

Aldred, Cyril. *Akhenaten Pharaoh of Egypt*. London, 1968
Badawy, Alexander. *Ancient Egyptian Architectural Design*. California, 1965
Carter, Howard. 'A Tomb Prepared for Queen Hatshepsut', *JEA* IV, 1917
Edgerton, William F. *The Tuthmosid Succession*. Chicago, 1933
Edgerton, William F. 'The Government and the Governed in the Egyptian Empire', *JNES*, 1947
Harris, James E. *et al. An X-Ray Atlas of the Royal Mummies*. Chicago, 1980
Helk, Wolfgang. *Das Bier in Alten Ägypten*. Berlin, 1971
Murnane, William J. *Ancient Egyptian Coregencies*. Chicago, 1977
Naville, Édouard. *Deir el Bahari*. 6 vols. London, 1894–1908
Romer, John. *Valley of the Kings*. London and New York, 1981
Winlock, Herbert E. *Excavations at Deir el Bahari, 1911–1931*. New York, 1942

CHAPTER TEN

Bleeker, C. J. *Egyptian Festivals*. Leiden, 1967
Eliot, T. S. *Four Quartets*. London, 1942
Fairman, H. W. 'The Kingship Rituals of Egypt' in *Myth, Ritual and Kingship*. Oxford, 1958
Hayes, William. *Royal Sarcophagi of the XVIII Dynasty*. Princeton, 1936
Piankoff, Alexandre. 'The Theology of the New Kingdom'. *Antiquity and Survival*, 6, 1956
Piankoff, Alexandre. *Egyptian Religious Texts and Representations*. 6 vols. Princeton, 1954–74
Ricke, Herbert. *Der Toten-Tempel Tuthmoses' III*. Cairo, 1939
Romer, John. 'Tomb of Tuthmosis III'. *MDAIK* 31,2, 1975

CHAPTER ELEVEN

Blackman, Aylward M. 'Some notes on the Ancient Egyptian Practice of Washing the Dead'. *JEA*, V, 1918
Blackman, Aylward M. 'The Rite of Opening the Mouth in Ancient Egypt and Babylon'. *JEA*, X, 1924
Bruyère, Bernard. *Les Fouilles de Deir el Médineh 1934–1935*. Cairo, 1939
Černý, Jaroslav. *A Community of Workmen at Thebes in the Ramesside Period*. Cairo, 1973
Černý, Jaroslav. *The Valley of the Kings*. Cairo, 1973

Janssen, Jac. J. *Commodity Prices from the Ramessid Period*. Leiden, 1975

CHAPTER TWELVE

Barguet, Paul. *Le Temple d'Amon-Rê à Karnak*. Cairo, 1962
Bell, Sir Harold Idris. *Egypt from Alexander the Great to the Arab Conquest*. Oxford, 1948
Bothmer, Bernard V. *Egyptian Sculpture of the Late Period*. Brooklyn, 1960
Cooney, John D. (ed.) *Coptic Egypt*. Brooklyn, 1944
Fairman, H. W. 'Worship and Festivals in an Egyptian Temple'. *Bull. John Rylands Library*, 37, Manchester, 1954
Glanville, S. R. K. (ed.) *The Legacy of Egypt*. Oxford, 1942
Kitchen, Kenneth A. *The Third Intermediate Period in Egypt*. Warminster, 1973
Meinardus, Otto F. A. *Christian Egypt: Ancient and Modern*. Cairo, 1977
Milne, J. Grafton. *A History of Egypt* (vol. 5 'Under Roman Rule'). London, 1898
Wilkinson, Sir John Gardner. *The Egyptians in the Time of the Pharaohs*. London, 1857

INDEX